I0127859

Ulla Dentlinger | Where are you from?

Lives
Legacies
Legends

⅃⊔⅃

**Lives
Legacies
Legends**

Ulla Dentlinger

Where are you from? | 'Playing White' under Apartheid

Basler Afrika Bibliographien | 2016

©the author
©the photographers
©Basler Afrika Bibliographien

A co-publication of:

Basler Afrika Bibliographien
PO Box
CH-4001 Basel
Switzerland
www.baslerafrika.ch

CARL SCHLETTWEIN
STIFTUNG

The Basler Afrika Bibliographien is part of the Carl Schlettwein Foundation

All rights reserved.

Most illustrations in this book are from the personal archive of Ulla Dentlinger. The recent photographs of Rehoboth in chapter two have been generously supplied by Cornelia Limpricht (Hamburg). Other photographs originate from the archives of the Evangelical Lutheran Church in the Republic of Namibia (ELCRN, Rehoboth Chronicle and Album) and the Basler Afrika Bibliographien (BAB, Dammann collection). Efforts were made to trace all copyright holders. We apologise for any incomplete or incorrect acknowledgements.

Cover photograph: Ulla around 1956 at Verlos or Namtses

Map on inside front cover: Apartheid and racial segregation in Namibia at a high point: the map of the so-called Odendaal plan which designated ethnic "homelands" to Namibia's African population. In the centre of the country the Rehoboth Gebiet. Adapted from the Report of the Commission of Enquiry into South West Africa Affairs 1962-1963. R.P. No 12/1964, Fig. 9

ISBN 978-3-905758-79-5

ISSN 1660-9638

Contents

In fond memory of my brave mother, Wilhelmine, and my strong sister, Ute. I would give anything to learn what details they would have added to my stories.

1 A TORMENTING QUESTION

People often have difficulty placing me. When I lived in the United States with my family, Oregonians were intrigued by my accent. They thought it sounded British. When we travel in Europe, nobody would suspect I am anything but European. In South Africa, people agree that I might be South African – but they also detect something indescribable that slightly sets me apart from them. When I switch into clear Afrikaans, they might smile in acceptance. But what takes the cake is when I speak a few sentences in Khoe, a local Namibian language. Now they become confused. "So, where are you actually from?" they will want to know.

To them this seems a simple, obvious question. Try as I might, I am not able to give them an equally short and simple answer. For me a whole lifetime is contained within that question. I have a story to tell, of which the gist is this: While growing up in rural Namibia in the mid-1950s, my parents did the unthinkable. Knowing we were of mixed heritage, yet wanting the best for their children as all good parents do, they arranged our schooling accordingly. They sent, first me and then later my sister, to white schools. Possibly encouraged by their initial success, all four of us went ahead and lived white lives. Had we now "jumped the colour line"? By various obscure and not well-documented processes – convinced they had to be secret – we believed we had changed our racial classification from "coloured" to that of "white". We juggled colour.

At the time, being white was a highly desirable status to have; in fact, it was *the* most desirable status. Now, some fifty years later – and twenty years after the dismantlement of apartheid – it becomes ever harder to say what advantage it brought us. As the world at large becomes ever more diverse, who can say it is better to belong to one group than to another? Who can today even categorically say: "I belong to ethnic group A, while my neighbour belongs to ethnic group B"? Do we even have to belong to groups?

At that time, though, this private family reclassification which we took upon ourselves was certainly not something done lightly. It was a step fraught with uncertainty, even danger. The price we paid was anguish, constant fear of detection and a sacrifice of family connectedness. The decades-long process of subsequently becoming comfortable with my new identity was psychologically so unnerving that I have only recently felt free to talk about it. This is certainly the first time I ever write about it.

On 21 March 1990 Namibia became independent, thereby officially ending its mandated status to South Africa. On 27 April 1994, apartheid was officially dismantled in South Africa, a result of the first free elections since 1948, with the African National Congress replacing the Nationalist Party. People born after these two dates (often called the "born free" generation) have thankfully been spared legal colour discrimination and are sometimes unable to relate to apartheid as it once existed. It is hard for them to imagine that only two decades ago there were certain schools for white children in South Africa and others for black children, that seating arrangements in buses or in trains were reserved according to colour, that certain jobs were allowed to some and certain salaries prohibited for others, that there were legally prescribed places to live and partners to choose from, all of which was determined by the tone of your complexion or the texture of your hair. Some older southern Africans have simply put these years behind them, wishing to forget. Foreigners, of course, feel outrage at the injustices suffered by black people, but might not quite understand the complex plight of those with mixed genetic background, who were equally victims of a harsh and inhumane policy.

Yet those of us who grew up as people of colour after the South African elections of 1948 that called the conservative Nationalist Party into life - and who subsequently saw discrimination based on colour being written into law - remember our heritage transformed from being a personal attribute to that of a public logo, permeating every fibre of our existence. In Namibia[1], too, people were now rigorously assigned to racial categories of white and non-white, and then more precisely into European, Owambo, Nama, Herero. And then, of course, came the category of mixed racial backgrounds, such as the Coloureds or the Basters. In fact, these groupings had already existed during German colonial times, but the South Africans now had the political apparatus to almost perfect their system of entrenching differences - but not absolutely. There remained grey areas. My family was to use these grey areas to their advantage during the early 1950s.

With this background in mind, consider for a moment the seemingly innocent question: "Where are you from?" The average respondent would happily, when asked about their background, proceed to give their country or place of birth, perhaps name the place they grew up in. They might talk about where they went to school, college or university, then continue to talk about their family, how earlier generations came to settle at a particular locality, possibly mention one or other memorable relative ... at any rate, go on a pleasant journey into their personal past. With the question answered, the average listener, no doubt, will now be keen to tell their own story, tell where they come from.

All of us have participated in this dance of questions and answers about our background. It is the way we probe someone we are getting newly acquainted with. If we run out of something intelligent to say, the question "Where do you come from?" breaks the ice at a party. It makes good small talk at a dinner table. It provides common ground between speakers and creates noted differences.

As a child on our Namibian farm, I learned early on that my family was not one to revel in stories of where we were from. My parents guarded even the most mundane details about their own parents much like a state secret. Innocent questions about their past from my sister and me would elicit – not smiles at the pleasure of reminiscing, needing no prompting to spill out – but instead, wary sideway glances hinting of the fear of detection. My father's standard response would be to remain stoic, while my mother looked hurt. These mysterious reactions would be followed by an awkward silence, best described as if a primary school student was being punished for some offence. A definite but inexplicable sense of guilt hung in the air. It was not altogether clear who the guilty party was meant to be: was it my sister or me, for asking? Or were my parents hiding some mystery too horrendous to be admitted? Why were they feeling so uncomfortable? Since nothing was verbalised, we all just let it pass. Finally, we stopped asking.

Modern psychologists would probably warn against this kind of parenting. Ignoring strange habits tends to perpetuate them in families and make them heritable legacies. Having been sensitised to these latent signals, my sister and I began to mimic this strange behaviour and then adopt it as our own. As young children, we would now, in turn, never willingly offer any information on the little we knew about our background. Instead we hunkered down, as our parents did, ducking apparently potentially embarrassing questions. Later as a teenager, should a conversation develop in the direction of parentage or heritage, I would silently cringe, instinctively wishing: "Oh, let's just move on to another subject and forget about this one". Finally, during my high school years I drew my own lonely conclusions. We had to be of mixed heritage – coloured – as such people were called in southern Africa. And living as whites, as we did, was against the law. But what else was there to do but continue as before – quietly, secretly – in line with the family tradition?

Not being able to speak for my sister, I can only assume that the full and powerful meaning must have hit her as hard as it did me. I know from friends that she was teased at school in Windhoek about her heritage. She seemed to have internalised and suffered so much from this "affliction" that, after her very early death from cancer, good friends finally summoned up the courage to ask me whether she had been abused. They had difficulty imagining what made her seem to bear some secret burden.

I feel that I was lucky to have avoided such acute suffering. Perhaps my personality was different; perhaps my subsequent distance from Namibia made it easier for me. From an early age I had been drawn to differences in people, an unusual look, foreign places. I intuitively gravitated towards the study of anthropology, hoping to explore "otherness". I was also keen on travelling. Getting married to a German and leaving South Africa, therefore, while making me wary at first, later seemed natural.

In April 1984, ten years before the end of apartheid and newly married, my husband and I left South Africa for green, lush Portland, Oregon. Oregonians, always ready to strike up a conversation, were intrigued by my accent. In the supermarket or on the street people would ask: "Where are you from?" In spite of now living in the United States, my gut response still was - run and hide! I steered clear of even mentioning Namibia. Instinctively, I would still ask myself, "What if somebody knows?" Since I had to provide some sort of answer, I would focus on the country of my later youth, South Africa, and speak of my education there. With blonde hair and green eyes, people probably thought of me as a true Afrikaner. I was in no frame of mind to tell them otherwise.

Later I would dare to say: "I was born in Namibia, but educated in South Africa." At first it would pass me by that I would have to explain where Namibia was, point out its German colonial roots, its mandated relationship to South Africa and its present struggle for independence as the last colony in Africa. It took a while to realise that this was the extent of people's interest in me. Predictably, they now went on to tell their own family story. "My grandfather was stationed in Morocco for a while during World War II ...", or "I had family in Africa. My uncle went to do missionary work in Malawi ..."

The closest Native American reservation to Portland was Warm Springs. I pressed my young family - by now it had grown by two boys - to visit there. At the time I believed my attraction to the reservation was academic. Now I sense there must have been deeper motives. I was happy in Oregon. Yet amid the forests and ferns, I must have longed for the wide-open, arid spaces of my childhood with the horizon visible. Warm Springs had that aridity, but it also had the poverty and neglect of those marginal rural communities familiar to me. Deep down it must have reminded me of the rural Namibia of my childhood. This interest had further consequences. Talking to Oregonians about Native Americans, I would secretly gulp when people would quite naturally say that they were part-Iroquois or Cheyenne or Navaho. I was surprised that they would admit this so freely.

Once our two sons had aged sufficiently and asked questions about my background, I wanted to answer these honestly. I finally became tired of beating around the bush and using euphemisms. They appeared not to be necessary. One day, the unthinkable happened: my answer to the next "where are you from?" simply was, "I was actually born in Rehoboth, Namibia, grew up on a farm with wide-open spaces and then lived in South Africa until I came here". I had to pinch myself to fathom that the characteristic heart flutter, the panic setting in, the constriction in the stomach did not appear. Since my darkest fear of being found out and having to admit and explain my background had never been realised, "where are you from?" had finally become a normal question for me as well.

Once I had become desensitised and free of panic, ever so slowly I continued admitting my heritage. With time, I occasionally even dared to explain my family history to one or the other close acquaintance. They were intrigued. It gave them a completely different picture of ethnicity in southern Africa – not one of black versus white, but one of shades of brown. With their "everybody can make it" approach to life, some considered it a success story. This certainly was a novel perspective for me. Some went further and suggested I write it down, seeing that apartheid was now dead and gone.

We left the States in 1997 to live in Germany. The children were older, and with Namibia only a night's flight away, I was now able to return at regular intervals. Having come out of the racial closet, I was curious to test my new approach on friends and family members there. I was surprised at how it had become quite the thing to admit to our kind of ancestry in South Africa. One of my cousins even played our story down, saying, "Many families experienced what we did. Some lost loved ones, suffering persecution and internment. Our dilemma was mild in comparison."

Her opinion did not discourage me. It raised further questions. If we were one of many, how then did others deal with these issues? I thought I would start asking my own family how they felt about the years prior to independence.

Every time I was in Namibia I looked up one or the other relative or close friend of the family. Some I knew vaguely from my early childhood, but others we had never visited again after the early 1960s. I wanted to hear what they had done with their lives, how they related to the question of our background, or simply ask them to fill in the gaps of my own memory. I was also curious how the country as a whole was dealing with a colour-free legal system. I began spending time in the rural area of Rehoboth where I had grown up. Many relatives joyfully opened their doors to me. In this way, I was again able, after many decades, to spend deeply meaningful time with a woman, Lena, who had been connected with my family for over fifty years. She had taught me Khoe as a child, was our all-round housekeeper, masseuse, healer and midwife in the area. I made sure to visit her each time I could, cherishing the memory of how she had indulged and teased us as children. I made a hasty trip to Namibia finally to attend her funeral – she had reached the age of one hundred and seven. On another visit, I made a recording of an aunt's story. My father's sister, Hedi, had told me about her run-in with the law decades ago. I had been drawn to her narrative then, but had forgotten the details of it. As she retold it, we both profited from the memory. I got to know my mother's family again. We had unfortunately rarely associated with

My mother during a stop on the way to the Kuiseb River, early 1984

them in my youth, but I knew them from my early preschool years. The process of researching my family background consequently came to involve other relatives. A previously known but subsequently ignored world presented itself to me once again. A sense of awe crept into my being. Did I actually belong to all of this, beyond my own immediate European-orientated family?

Today, some fifty years after my childhood in poor, rural Namibia, should I find myself at a party or a dinner table and someone asks me where I come from, I cannot help but smile inwardly. I will now say, with true anticipation, something like: "I was born in Namibia, in a place called Rehoboth, was educated in South Africa and then from there just went out into the world". I will lean back and wait. Some people will pass over my reply, oblivious of its meaning to me. Others will delve and, on occasion, this becomes interesting to me on a level they are totally unaware of. For it has taken me virtually a lifetime of probing, questioning, self-analysis and particularly research, to arrive at the point of admitting my heritage. Since then I have come to realise that our particular background in southern Africa was nourished with a richness of indigenous humour, a variety of local languages and a spread of customs. After having denied my family saga for so long, I have finally come to embrace and declare it my own. Like everyone else, I now feel that my background, too, is special. More than that, though, I feel more honest, giving credit to members of my wider family who were courageous and had integrity. I curiously and belatedly feel one with them. Most people are naturally drawn to their heritage – perhaps not to every detail thereof – but to its overall personal uniqueness. Now, finally, I feel about my heritage much like everybody else feels about theirs.

So, to those family members of mine who continue to hide from our mixed genetic background, I can only say that the biological differences between us are negligible. A political system, for its own benefit, chose to emphasise colour to divide people. With that system now gone, we are free to decide by ourselves who we want to be and what we want to call ourselves, if anything at all. Why not confront history? It really pays. It is truly liberating[2]. Not only does it liberate, it also connects. It connects one to places, people and times. And that feels good; so good that, I believe, it is this feeling of connectedness which makes people want to talk about their heritage, of whatever kind it might be.

2 REHOBOTH... COLOURFUL AND CONTROVERSIAL

When confronting history for answers to my own heritage, I came to realise that my search must begin with happenings at the Cape of Good Hope, nearly two thousand kilometres south of Rehoboth about four centuries ago. Of course textbooks, novels, and historical accounts proliferate regarding the arrival of Europeans in southern Africa, but become fewer on events of later periods further away from the Cape. Yet these historical events culminated in making me and others the people we are today.

This chapter begins with a detailed description and discussion of Rehoboth, my birthplace. From there, the focus widens onto the history of southern Africa and factors that led to the situation of discrimination based on colour, before narrowing the lens once again. For those who are interested, I have endnoted many additional facts for further reference.

Rehoboth lies in the centre of Namibia on the B1, the national road which is the main artery of the country as a whole, as it runs from the Orange River on its southern national border to Ondangwa on its northern national border. Gravel roads fan out from the B1, linking it to the *Gebiet* (as its surrounding area is still called), and in the west to the beautiful Oanob Dam Reserve, exclusive residential area popular with locals as well as Europeans. It links south-west to the copper mine at Klein Aub and to farms beyond, and in the south-east to Uhlenhorst and yet more farms. Just a few kilometres outside town alongside the railway line is the railway station, still rather obviously called Bahnhof, the German equivalent of "station".

Most people approach Rehoboth from the capital Windhoek, which lies eighty-seven kilometres north. As you leave Windhoek, the B1 winds through the picturesque Auas Mountains. The geomorphology shows off smooth hills with rocky tops alternating with expansive plains with clusters of acacia groves. You will pass newly developed exclusive residential areas, a retire-

Approaching Rehoboth on the B1. Photographer: Cornelia Limpricht

ment and conference centre, the railway siding and former hotel of Aris, as well as the local well-known farm school and a stone quarry, before the road becomes a long straight stretch. The mountains will then drop back to the east and the west as the terrain flattens out. Farm settlements lie scattered on either side. Still continuing south, several world-class lodges and resorts have opened along the route. Inviting entrances of elaborate stone structures might encourage you to come this way again. Soon afterwards the vegetation changes into a bushy highland savannah.

About here, during a late or dry summer season, one of little rain, you might have to slow down for the odd donkey or small herd of goats enjoying the last yellow tufts of grass between the road and the farm fence. As the B1 extends straight ahead, its endpoint merging with the horizon, you are able to glance at the isolated cattle or goat post with decimated pasture to your left and right. You may become seriously concerned about the degree of aridity and the extent of overgrazing, even finding yourself muttering in disbelief: "How do people and animals manage to survive? How could it have come to this bad state?"[3]

By contrast, in a year blessed with abundant summer rains, the opposite is true: the undulating Auas Mountains will be covered with a carpet of green. This low-growing, fast-appearing grass cover will accompany you all the way into the town of Rehoboth itself and beyond. Then the klapper bushes[4] will be in bloom, as will the numerous acacia trees. Cattle will show off shiny coats of brown. The goats will be wandering purposefully from bush to bush. Farmyards will be sitting snugly amid the green. Your drive will be enjoyable, perhaps even memorable.

You will have almost made it when you see the sign for Oanob Dam on the edge of town. Still on the B1 you will pass a middle-class residential area to your east. The majority of the houses are moderately sized, many in a state of semi-completion. The next noticeable structure on the same side of the B1 is the Dr Lemmer High School, one of many schools of Rehoboth. You can hardly miss the obviously grander houses to the west. Opulent and surrounded by green gardens, they hug the foot of the hills. Here, wealth is evident in stark contrast to the poorer, smaller houses with barren yards, lying lower once again to the east.

Two splendid petrol stations have recently appeared on the east side of the B1. They give an impression of bustling trade with spanking new pumps and wide stopping-berths. At one of the stations, eleven metal plates present historical facts on the area and town, written by Dr Cornelia Limpricht, an historian and long-time supporter of the community, and donated by a well-known Namibian organisation.

Also on the east side of the B1, Rehoboth now shows off a mall in Block F, a subsection of town. This is a vast improvement on the shopping conditions of my youth, from which I remember virtually only a *smous* (itinerant trader) and local butchery alongside the Prosopis[5] trees. Now some well-known chain stores and restaurants make shopping and dining a lot easier for Rehobothers, who used to have to drive all the way to Windhoek.

Proceed southwards on the main road. Turn left. Until a few years ago, you would have been able to quench your thirst at what once was the first petrol station in the town. But now it is closed, falling into disrepair. In stark contrast to the two new stations, it has become an eyesore at the entrance to the town.

Should you approach Rehoboth from the south, you will experience one of the most beautiful scenes in Namibia, the reason why the German colonial power was once so keen to lay its hands on the Rehoboth territory. You are quite likely to see a donkey cart, its axles moaning, laden with farm employees and their supplies on their way back to the farms, the driver's whip sticking up like a flagpost into the air. You will cross the Oanob River, pass through the outskirts of town and end up at the same deserted petrol station.

Taking the first tarred road from here into town will give you an initial impression of the community. During weekends of reasonable temperatures, you will feel a pleasant throb hard to resist. Vendors will be selling their *koeksusters*, *roosterbrood* or *vetkoek* – sugary pastries cooked in heated oil or meat fried on the open fire – sending out billowing clouds of smoke and mouth-watering smells. Children will be calling to each other across the roads, music blaring from cruising cars, people mulling around in small groups in front of Woermann and Brock supermarket, talking and laughing. This is Rehoboth at its homeliest. The throng of shoppers will become a

*Rehoboth in 2011.
Photographer:
Cornelia Limpricht*

stream at the height of shopping hours, particularly on a late Saturday morning. The same hustle and bustle is evident at the local Spar supermarket just a few streets away.

With each successive visit, I have noticed an increasing number of vendors trading from stands, offering fruit, vegetables and cheap Chinese items. If it was in my power to improve the physical appearance of the town, I might have concentrated these vendors in an open-air market at some central place offering those mouth-watering grilled delicacies together with some home industry items as an attraction for passing tourists. Rehoboth has no major industry to speak of. Most businesses are service-orientated. Economically it is carried by the farming industry of the surrounding area. It is known for its artisans, mostly builders who take their expertise out of the town primarily to Windhoek, as do other professionals, notably teachers, engineers and public servants. Few trained or educated men and women find employment in the town.

All of this might sound like your average small town anywhere in the world, with pleasant and unpleasant aspects. Often in rural towns in America, houses are in disrepair and open unkempt areas line some streets. Many German towns, though attractive from a distance, seem to be almost deserted on closer inspection. The same applies to many French villages even in popular rural districts. On the surface, Rehoboth seems no exception. I know, however, that there is much more to this town than meets the eye. Looking deeper, not only do contradictions appear, but also some surprisingly controversial features. My life was influenced by these very contradictions and controversies.

If it's hot, you will hang onto your cold drink for as long as possible. The heat in Rehoboth can be formidable. Is it because of one's discomfort then, that the unpleasant aspects of Rehoboth are emphasised – the dust in the streets, the manner in which people trudge along, the way inebriated men are seen slouching in doorways? Emaciated dogs will look for a spot of shade. Dirty children play in the streets. This is the unspectacular Rehoboth. In his masters thesis written in the mid-1980s, Pearson[6] says of the visual aspect of Rehoboth: "The town presents a fairly bleak picture to the visitor." Since then, not much has changed, even though the town has grown noticeably.

Many residents of wider Namibia would consider "unspectacular and bleak" to be a kind description. "Rehoboth – I wouldn't want to be buried there!" is what I heard someone say some years ago. This is a damning opinion. Sad as it is for insiders to hear, this is how the outside world at times observes the town. In spite of the odd improvement, the casual visitor might notice that there are street lamps along the main road that is actually tarred. But any side road remains a stretch of gravel, pocked with potholes, garbage along the shoulder in the absence of sidewalks. There are no water drainage channels. Pearson wrote of the town: "Its streets are untarred swathes of sand: dusty, usually corrugated, and without street lights".[7] Once again the casual visitor might ask: "What happens to people's taxes?" or "Where is the municipality? What is it doing?" The visitor may mentally start improving conditions: "I'd encourage them to open an ice cream stand", or "I would re-open the swimming pool", or "What about a town square with trees and maybe a fountain to create an impression of coolness?"

Even Rehobothers who love their town cannot help noticing its short-comings such as the obvious dearth of entertainment. Dr Cornelia Limpricht, author of many historical articles and the latest comprehensive book on Rehoboth, notes that there are "hardly any appropriate recreational oppor-tunities for young people between the ages of 15 and 25".[8] To date, this con-dition has not changed. I am told that lately, young people have taken to spo-radically "hanging out together" at an empty plot in town to provide their own sort of entertainment. Otherwise young people in search of some excitement over the weekend will drive the eighty-seven kilometres to Windhoek for a night on the town. These Saturday night outings have been known to end badly, as the stretch of the B1 between Windhoek and Rehoboth has a high accident rate. In the past, ways were found to entertain adoles-cents. Older residents tell how a church hall would double as a cinema. In the 1950s, the horseracing track outside town provided a reason for a healthy social gathering of residents. Both these sources of entertainment no long-er exist. The horseracing track is a ruin. Perhaps the new mall with its res-taurants will now offer something in terms of entertainment.

Rehoboth has so much potential. And it has a rich history, a part of which has been discovered and made public by outsiders, while residents have also contributed. Searching for iron ore smelting sites in 1969, Namibian archae-ologist Dr Beatrice Sandelowsky was shown such a site by two local residents on the edge of town. She describes the search and subsequent excavation of the Drierivier site.[9] The excavation was followed by fundraising to develop further adventurous projects in the area. One of these was an aerial survey of Rehoboth and its vicinity, funded by the Rössing Foundation of Namibia. In the process, more archaeological sites were discovered along the banks of the Oanob River. Seven excavated stone cairns held skeletons in foetal posi-tion, the traditional Khoe-San burial posture. One of these, a two-hundred-year-old burial, was restored and enclosed by an outdoor monument[10] as a memorial to the original people of the area and a gift to the inhabitants of Rehoboth. A fellow anthropologist, Antje Otto, and I, together with our young children at the time, visited the site shortly before its completion. It was a structure of elegant design enclosing the burial behind glass, where stairs opposite provided sitting and standing space, or simply space for reflection and enjoyment. Unfortunately, this monument has since fallen into neglect and become dilapidated.

With the help of her local and international team, Dr Sandelowsky founded a museum and library during the 1980s, providing a platform for numerous educational events seminars, training courses, and the granting of bursaries to students. Sadly, most of these activities have been terminated for multiple and complex reasons.

Rehoboth has so many resources. As already mentioned, the vegetation and geomorphology surrounding Rehoboth is exquisitely beautiful. Dr Limpricht has pointed out how this, not to mention its history, could be used as an advertisement for Rehoboth. With a little planning and a minimum of organisation, obvious resources could become profitable tourist attractions. One local resource she mentions is the huge acacia forest, a large collection of grand and ancient trees, nationally protected. Some are said to be as old as two thousand years. With some fencing and gates, staffing and marketing, the forest could raise revenues for the town. In its immediate vicinity, the Drierivier historical burials could be refurbished and included in a walking trail. In countries elsewhere in the world, such an asset would long since have been used to show off the town and, on top of it, earn some revenue. Instead, in Rehoboth there is no supervision of who enters the forest and removes the wood to burn as cooking fuel.[11]

Surprisingly, Rehoboth has more than fifty churches in a community of only about thirty thousand people.[12] This reflects the deep religious nature of Rehobothers, a phenomenon reaching back to their historical roots. Church activities shape social life. In spite of efforts to unite denominational groups, however, the large number of churches, each desiring individual independence has resulted in competition between them. Certain authors on Rehoboth have suggested this possibly to be one reason for "the deplorable state of affairs". Churches divide the community, stopping the residents speaking with one voice on matters relating to municipal issues.[13]

Particularly if one knows something about Rehoboth's history, would it not be justified to ask what has happened to the far-sightedness of Rehobothers when they first compiled a draft of their own constitution in 1868? Where is the courage that once made them take on the mighty German army at Sam Kubis, or oppose the South African Union in 1923?[14] Does it not seem that this proud community, which once stood up to the Cape government, has become somewhat complacent?

Rehoboth is controversial for reasons of poverty, divisiveness of the community, and an apparent lack of concerted involvement of community members. This seems to be the case, in spite of the fact that Rehoboth has a number of notably rich residents and certainly capable individuals – and more than its fair share of educated, well-positioned and well-intending indi-

Rehoboth in 2010.
Photographer:
Cornelia Limpricht

viduals, who are also leaders in the community. Again, one could argue that this cluster of elements can be found in many such towns anywhere in the world, and that conditions are often related to the politics of the society at large. They are not exceptional to Rehoboth; certainly the reasons for them are multiple and not always a result of the shortcomings of its residents. However, in the light of the present political status quo in Namibia as a whole, the community is playing into the hands of those who have always looked upon it with critical eyes, if not actually looked down on it.

In addition and sadly, the apparent lack of community engagement diverts away from the attractions Rehoboth has to offer and underplays the courageous efforts of isolated individuals to improve conditions. Unless one gets to know some residents well, one will never see the really attractive and tidily kept homes. At Sam Kubis, the well-known battle against the German colonial occupying force is annually re-enacted, complete with a procession of women and men in traditional costumes. The local well-known artist Andrew van Wyk, whose works are to be found in many places, runs an art school and gallery where he trains students in the basics of sketching and drawing. The art school was, for me, a truly pleasant and unexpected surprise. I spoke to Andrew some years back as he elaborated on his plans for extension. And then I saw one of his pieces at Basler Afrika Bibliographien in Basel, Switzerland, and was perfectly amazed and speechless with pride for my birthplace.

One can feel pride one moment, and despair in the next. No sooner has a project been started, than it is abandoned. Some years back, a small group of enterprising young women planted trees on the traffic islands of major roads in the centre of town, as if to say: "We are proud of our town and we will show our pride, irrespective of what might happen". They were positively surprised that not all the trees had been uprooted during the first night after their planting!

Rehoboth is therefore not only colourful, but it is also contradictory. It is a pity that these and similar efforts are not effective in diminishing the unfortunately disagreeable reaction that even neutral travellers experience when passing through the town. Even Rehobothers themselves see their town critically. Therefore, when asked "Where do you come from?" they might hesitate to readily say with pride: "I come from Rehoboth".

Apart from its picturesque geography and some social issues, Rehoboth is best known for a completely different reason. In fact, anyone with any interest in what are colloquially called "mixed race issues" will immediately recognise the name. I would say it is the quintessential mixed race community in southern Africa, a colourful crowning product of mating between people of differing physical appearances and origins over the centuries. For one, the history of the subcontinent is reflected in the languages spoken here.

The official and most widely spoken language in Rehoboth is Afrikaans, followed by Khoekhoegowab (Khoe for short) as spoken by the Nama, the Namibian indigenous subgroup of the Khoe and the Dama people.[15] The third most frequently used language is English. The Afrikaans spoken in Rehoboth has its own particular nuances. The way people pronounce certain words sets local Afrikaans apart from South African Afrikaans. For instance, "Rehoboth" becomes shortened to "Repport", as both vowels and consonants are contracted. Our family name, Dentlinger, will have the first "e" lengthened, slurred into a twang, making it sound more like "De-anlinger" with the "t" disappearing altogether and the "g" softened. This slurring of vowels reminds me of the manner in which French speakers around the Mediterranean will nasalise some vowels and extend others, making it difficult, even for Parisians to understand at times.

Khoe terms are easily, often humorously, incorporated into Afrikaans either in a translated form or as is. For instance, from my childhood I remember mostly elderly Afrikaans speakers punctuating specific points in their stories with *"die Heer(rrr)e weet"*. As they raised their tone and rolled the "r", they tried to stress the truthfulness of their statement. "Die Here weet" is the translation of "as God is my witness". Its easy and frequent use, I believe, could be directly appropriated from the Khoe *"Ti Elob ao"*, vocative "my God!" or "as true as God", a popular appeal as to the veracity and seriousness of one's statements. Khoe was spoken as fluently as Afrikaans by most of the older residents when I was a child. Still today, individual Khoe words are incorporated into Afrikaans, even by the younger generation.

They might use the Khoe "/naa" (meaning "good") in a normal Afrikaans sentence, emphasising their enjoyment of something. Similarly, the Khoe term "!Garinîga" (Afrikaans "stigters", English "founders") is used in its Khoe form in daily speech and describes those families who came to Rehoboth in the first of several migrations. In my observation, the use of this word will often be accompanied by a kind of embarrassed, self-deprecating laughter. I think people laugh at themselves for using a Khoe term. They might believe its use signifies backwardness and being old-fashioned, yet they use it and then laugh at themselves for doing so. They might also feel slightly embarrassed using a Khoe term, since speakers of this indigenous language are considered lower in social status. Finally "/Annes", the Khoe name of Rehoboth, (meaning "smoky" or "misty" and referring to the steam rising from the former hot springs), is as often used as its biblical counterpart, Rehoboth, from Genesis 26:22.[16]

The Khoe language and culture was an integral part of my childhood. It influenced and shaped my life in many subtle, but also overt ways. I have internalised many values emanating from this culture and, in my middle age, I am grateful for this influence.

The history of the subcontinent is also evident in the faces of the people in the streets and on the farms. The genetic and cultural mix of Rehobothers, for many Namibians, is their defining characteristic. "This is how we identify the Rehoboth Basters, by their mixed background," people might say, even those holding no prejudice.

Looking at the colour of people's complexion in the streets, their hair texture and the colour of their eyes, we have to admit that Rehobothers reflect an extremely wide range. Their skin colour is anything from gentle peaches and cream to a deep rich African black. Natural hair texture can be cascading blonde to tight, dark brown peppercorn tufts and all the textures in-between. Their eye colour may be black or blue or brown. A cursory impression of people in the street already makes it clear that categorising Rehobothers according to any genetic indicators is a futile attempt.

Possibly towns such as Rehoboth would not exist today if in the fifteenth century, Portuguese and Dutch explorers had not come to the southernmost tip of Africa by sea from Europe. It was the age of discovery of new continents and cultures, and particularly of the resources that these newly discovered cultures offered. Mostly these voyages of discovery were commercial in nature. And all along the coast from the southernmost tip of Africa to present-day Namibia, European sailors came across coastal dwellers with olive skin and short, curly, dark hair.

By the end of the sixteenth century, the Dutch increasingly stopped over at the Cape. Then in 1652 the directors of the Dutch East India Company sent Jan van Riebeeck to establish a refreshment station there, "to regularize the benefits that sailors had long derived from the Cape stopover".[17] One of the benefits referred to was trade with the local pastoral Khoe: meat for their scurvy-invested sailors in exchange for tobacco, alcohol, iron and copper.

Less than two months after his arrival at the Cape, Van Riebeeck decided that he would need help with the physical work. The garrison of less than two hundred men in the first decade was insufficient for all the tasks to be done, particularly for building the fort. In line with the thinking of the day, he wrote to Batavia that slaves would be useful for "the dirtiest and heaviest work".[18] As an accepted source of manual labour, slavery became a pre-ordained consequence of the settlement at the Cape. Over the years, Madagascar became the source of most of these slaves, with India and Indonesia each contributing a smaller number.[19] By 1834 at the time of the slaves' emancipation, their number had risen to more than thirty-six thousand at the Cape.[20]

The introduction of slavery is obviously directly related to the resulting cultural and ethnic mix we find in southern Africa today. Once the slave lodge at the bottom of Cape Town was completed in 1679, this is where the company slaves would live under the supervision of overseers. It is a well-established fact that the lodge became a sort of a prostitution house, not only for sailors of passing ships, but also for local men.[21] Some officials were concerned about the degree of miscegenation, but their attempts to keep European men away from slave women bore little fruit.[22] Even though there is debate on how many children of ethnic mix were born to female lodgers, the fact remains that it was centrally situated in Cape Town and was an obvious attraction for up to fifty thousand company soldiers and sailors who disembarked there between 1701 and 1710, all with money in their pockets and only a brief time to spend it.[23] Consequently, at least half the number of children born to company slave women between 1671 and 1693 had European fathers.[24] In spite of the large number of children born out of wedlock, there were also a few cases of official marriages between slave women and European men during the seventeenth century.[25]

Meanwhile, local life took its own turn. The main reason for the establishment of the station in 1652 by van Riebeeck had been to start agriculture at the southern tip of Africa, the belief being that this was an extremely fertile area. His first agricultural attempts, however, did not turn out as had been anticipated. Contemplating his failure, van Riebeeck argued that independent farmers would do better with agriculture than employees of the company. He therefore suggested to the company that private persons might be given land to farm on independently. So, in February 1657, parcels of land were allocated to free *burghers* (citizens) at Rondebosch,[26] all of whom remained subjects but not employees of the company.

In my understanding, it is the granting of freehold land that set the ball rolling for increasing numbers of agrarian and later pastoral settlers to move away from the present Cape Flats, ever further into the north-western Cape and beyond, where they finally settled. There they and their often mixed-heritage descendants created settlements, villages and communities, the remnants of whom are still present today.

Thus, when Simon van der Stel relieved van Riebeeck in 1679, he arrived with orders to begin new expansion.[27] This he did by granting freehold land in the Stellenbosch area and beyond. Land not claimed for cultivation could be used by the free burghers for rough grazing.[28] In principle, at the beginning of the eighteenth century, land could readily be acquired in a number of ways by interested farmers.[29] This was easier if they were white, as we shall see soon. All cultivators also owned stock (cattle and sheep), which they let graze on public land. The further inland settlers moved, the more stock farming replaced cultivation. This was augmented with the hunting of game that was found in great abundance in the western Cape. By 1750 Europeans came to settle in Namaqualand not simply as ivory hunters or livestock traders or raiders, but on loan farms. This continued right up to the Orange River at Goodhouse.[30]

As this expansion continued, the burghers needed additional labour. Partly this was supplied by importing more slaves, but increasingly the Khoe-San, the original residents of the plains and mountains into which the settlers were thrusting their advance, became part of frontier society. Especially the Khoe were forced into labour on frontier farms by legal means, such as the requirement to carry passes. Consequently, mostly on the frontier, the Khoe increasingly became part of European culture, not only culturally but also biologically.

Except for a few cases,[31] it was only later[32] that European men would intermarry with Khoe women. Far away from Cape authorities and critical eyes of neighbours, the frontiersmen would - more as a rule, than the exception - have liaisons of varying kinds with local Khoe women, which rarely led to marriage.[33] Information on such unions is scanty. However, it is generally accepted by researchers that about ten per cent of all Cape marriages between 1700 and 1795 were mixed.[34] As for the slaves, because the males significantly outnumbered the females slaves,[35] many of them found marriage partners among the Khoe women. Thereby they created a new kind of progeny.

The first marriage between a free burgher[36] and a black woman took place in 1686. By 1695, a total of twelve European settlers had married black women in the newly opened areas of Stellenbosch and Drakenstein.[37] Black-Khoe liaisons mostly occurred after 1670 on European-owned farms where black slaves and Khoe worked together.[38] The descendants of these liaisons between individuals of different heritage were collectively called "bastaards". It goes without saying that this name was imported from Europe.

Nigel Penn[39] describes how these particular individuals were treated and what their status was. He tells us that children resulting from the first type of relationship, namely between Europeans and slaves, were dealt with depending on the case. For instance, if the European father acknowledged the offspring as his child, such individuals could secretly or even openly be incorporated into the Cape community. The former reporter now turned prolific writer, Max du Preez,[40] actually describes several official marriages of European men with slave women. The children from these unions were considered to be outside the normal discriminatory norms.

The "bastaard" progeny of a match between a European and a Khoe was ostensibly free, depending on such factors as the status of the parents or family and the social climate in which they lived. They might have simply been incorporated into the colonial society.

The offspring of the third type of union, namely that between a slave and a Khoe, were called "Bastaard-Hottentot". They were considered the lowest in the social ladder.[41] In practical terms, this kind of classification could not have lasted long. By 1731 the white population was already native born.[42] Increasingly, though, "bastaards" of all kinds experienced discrimination and ostracism, extending to blatant persecution and even death. Accordingly, by the end of the eighteenth century the conditions of the Khoe "were no better than that of a 'Bastaard-Hottentot' or a slave".[43] Many Khoe fled the Cape if they could – along with slaves fleeing bondage, debtors, escaped murderers, bandits, and vagabonds hiding from the law.[44]

The ethnic mixing continued as, company settlers increasingly moved northwards with their stock and settled on loan farms. All were in search of a better life, "turning their eyes to the naked plains of the interior, seeing themselves lords of their own lives".[45] The plains they fled to were the open territory beyond the control of the company, also called the "northern frontier". Generally speaking, his frontier covered any expanse between the Cape and the Orange River in the far north, where migrating settlers met local communities. It became a crucible for refugees of all kinds, adventurers, criminals, and raiders. However, as these wanderers were soon to find out, the northern plains were anything but naked.

From the earliest days of Dutch settlement at the Cape, the colonists had known about the existence of the Namaqua further north. Now they encountered them, as well as the hunting-gathering San, some of whom were still following their nomadic ways. Alongside these traditional communities and in time, new communities had formed, many of mixed racial composition. Although no detailed reports exist regarding the degree of intermingling of people of diverse backgrounds at the time, I think it is safe to conclude that the northern frontier was a complex composition of communities, freedom of movement of individuals, and a lack of law.

Again, Nigel Penn and others bring to life the conditions of lawlessness and anarchy that existed in the absence of any initial police presence, law of court or regulations prescribing relationships and interaction. From him we learn that raids and robberies were the order of the day. Chaos prevailed where violence often spoke louder than reason or sense – a veritable African Wild West. Predatory commando gangs robbed weaker groups of their livestock.[46] The Cape government tried to extend its control into the area, first with the appointment of *veldkorporaals* and later with the formation of Boer commandos instructed to establish a semblance of order. As best as they could, or according to their own personal discretion, they exercised their power and willy-nilly meted out justice, most often to the detriment of the original San and Khoe communities.[47]

How does this relate to Rehoboth? It does so in two ways. First, from the wreckage of disrupted earlier communities and finding strength in numbers, people with common interests would pool their resources and form new groups alongside groups that had existed previously. The groups themselves might split and dissolve again. Occasionally, though, they would remain and develop into a more permanent organisation, settling at a more or less distinctly defined area in the northern Cape. Some even developed a political, legal structure, referred to by historians as polities. One such group would become the forerunner of the present-day Rehobothers.

Other similar groups of individuals of varying backgrounds would leave Little Namaqualand and move beyond this natural border.[48] Historians refer to these groups collectively as the Oorlam. They were said to speak Dutch, own horses and guns, and were formed on the basis of a commando system, being well equipped to raid other cattle owners. At times they owned small herds that they depended on for sustenance, but mainly they were mobile raiders.[49]

Other loosely structured communities which formed on the Cape frontier at the time, have become known as the Basters. There were three such groups.[50] The Vilander Basters, under their leader Dirk Vilander, settled north of the Orange River at Rietfontein-Mier. Yet another community was that of the Gordonia Basters, settling at what is now Upington, but they were soon afterwards incorporated into Bechuanaland under the British government. Finally there were the de Tuin Basters, who later settled at Rehoboth[51] and have survived there to the present day. The Basters, too, were a collection of families and individuals of differing cultural and genetic backgrounds, continually incorporating a variety of individuals into their newly-formed ranks. In contrast to the Oorlam, however, they were primarily interested in stock farming with fat-tailed sheep for consumption, for which they needed land.[52]

Stock farming for human consumption had been the popular means of farming for most farmers in the northern Cape until the 1860s. However, as Pearson writes, from this time onwards, the British government in the Cape began to support wool farming instead, hoping to make it an item of national export and thereby recoup state income from the collapse of the wine industry. Wool farming, however, presupposed a different system of land tenure to mobile subsistence farming. Thus, the system of granting grazing licences which had been operative since 1846, was increasingly replaced by the leasing or sale of crown land. Rapidly, local pastoral communities were pushed aside, losing their land to white farmers with more commercial farming experience, and more networks and investment potential. Ultimately, many former subsistence farmers ended up as employees to the new breed of capitalist investors.[53]

Fearing these conditions might endanger their lives as well, the de Tuin people tried to pre-empt such developments. Pearson writes that "they petitioned the Divisional Council of Calvinia, within the borders of which de Tuin was situated, for a grant of land for their exclusive occupation. The Council rejected the request as 'impertinent' ".[54] Following this rejection, members of the de Tuin community decided to petition the Governor of the Cape directly.[55] In the petition they spoke of their long occupation of this part of the country and their forming a safe boundary between "marauding parties" to the north and the colonial farmers further south.[56] But their honest attempt to acquire land was apparently simply ignored.

This was not the end, though. Pressure on land increased along with the state of lawlessness and anarchy. Their desperation was raised to a pitch by stock thefts.[57] Finally, the decision was taken[58] that they would leave the Cape colony and migrate further northwards into what is now southern Namibia, then called Great Namaqualand. On 16 November 1868 they crossed the Orange River, as had the Afrikaner Oorlam and many others before them. Mostly these families remained together until they reached their final destination in Rehoboth.

It is perhaps because Rehobothers themselves turn the account of their northward migration into a trek of mythical proportions, that it has become a favourite topic of discussion for historians writing about Rehoboth.[59] However, details of their trek are not as important to my biographical sketches as are the details of historical background, the philosophy of the day regarding people of colour, and the social consequences of these. It is central to my narrative that a society developed in which genetics and colour came to be used to categorise individuals, first socially and then politically.

Of course this practice was not born on our soil, but is itself a consequence of political events and philosophical ideals far removed from southern Africa.

A point of departure for ethnic prejudice and discrimination would have been slavery, starting in the 1500s. Slaves were considered equivalent to material possessions, having virtually no culture of their own – or, if they had any, it was certainly considered inferior. They had no humanity.[60] It was now easy for discrimination to be extended to all people of colour who did not match the ideal of being blonde, light-skinned, hygienic and Catholic. As white expansion progressed, Khoe-San and then "bastaards" of all hews came to be considered as inferior, initiating a racially stratified view of people. At the tip of the pyramid was white society, followed in descending order by people of increasingly dark skin colour. For those on the lower rungs of this social ladder, privileges and access to resources fell in direct proportion to the rise in discrimination. This is very much the way in which broader white Namibian society continues to regard Rehoboth.

The second way in which this history relates to Rehoboth, is that my own family history reaches back to these chaotic but seminal historical processes of the eighteenth and nineteenth centuries. In my family, the men were of European extract, having come to Namibia as colonisers and having chosen to take local women as partners during the times and events described above.

Thus at the end of the nineteenth century, my German paternal great-grandfather, Gustav Dentlinger, married a woman from the south of Namibia called Sabina Olivier. From her looks and name, it is very likely that she was a progeny of Cape Dutch Malay – the pairing of Dutch men with female slaves which had become so prevalent in the Cape and western part of South Africa. Unfortunately no written records exist of her genealogical background. Family members relate that she came to the Orange River area from Kimberley. She is said to have left Kimberley because of racial discrimination. There is no way of telling how she came to live there. She probably was a product of the same maelstrom of conditions described above. Any written record of her was lost in fighting, raiding, racial interbreeding, mobility and illiteracy. Present-day Rehoboth Oliviers know of her, of course, but it was impossible to find anyone who could tell more than that she came from Kimberley.

A generation later, my maternal German grandfather took a partner called Susanna Bezuidenhout. The same applies to her. With a Dutch surname and having grown up in the Bethanie area close to the Fish River, it is not unlikely that her family belonged to those mixed individuals who had come to live in that area. She and my maternal grandfather, Enssle, moved to just south-west of Rehoboth to the farm Gamis, where their later children were born. Sadly again, no family records exist to prove that she was an off-spring of unions between Dutch men and indigenous Khoe women, but her name and her looks strongly suggest this. This is the ancestral background of the women in my genealogy several generations back. The background of the German men of the same generations is steeped in Namibian history at the turn of nineteenth and twentieth centuries, a topic to which I will return.

In retrospect, when people asked me as an adolescent where I came from, I could have given them this account of my historical roots. This might have led to a fascinating conversation. I had learned during my studies in Anthropology at the University of Cape Town that similar nation-building in conjunction with genetic mixing has taken place everywhere in the world. The chances are that an astute listener might have made this connection, or offered similar examples of historical racial mixing in his or her family. However, as an adolescent, I lacked the insight, the maturity, and perhaps the courage to respond in this way. I had not yet been desensitised. That only happened in the States, years later. Also, because apartheid had done such an efficient job labelling anything other than white as inferior, I feared admitting to my background. Even Rehobothers themselves have adopted the assumption that lighter is better. Regrettably, it took me years to work through my inhibitions regarding my multicultural and genetically mixed heritage.

Up to this day, Rehobothers are referred to as the Rehoboth Basters. Admittedly they also refer to themselves as such. Being aware of the historical facts as presented above, I became uneasy with the use of the term "Baster" for the residents of Rehoboth, and also with "Basterland" to describe the rural area surrounding the town. Many authors on the subject maintain that Baster is not related to the word "bastard". I find this linguistically hard to accept.

I also question the assertion that Rehobothers chose this name for themselves. Admittedly, the few Rehobothers I questioned about how they like to refer to themselves, spontaneously said, "I am a Rehoboth Baster," some adding, "and proudly so!" However, I rather think that the name was imposed upon them by immigrant Europeans during the seventeenth and eighteenth centuries, and has remained stuck. At least adding the town's name gives the title a geographical flavour, but "Baster" has always carried negative connotations, a suggestion of illegitimacy, of being excluded. Through the ages the term has had derogatory implications, originally referring to anyone who was not Catholic. At the very least it excludes people from the mainstream of society; at the worst it is an insult or swearword. I wish we could reconsider its use. Who would, under normal circumstances, willingly call themselves a bastard?

I have noticed English-speakers stumbling over the word, as if they actually strain to utter it. Reverend Jesse Jackson even takes offence at the term "slave" in his statement: "My great-great-grandmother was my great-great-grandmother; but for someone, she was a slave." [61] The point Jackson is making is that he cannot refer to his great-great-grandmother as a slave. I have to agree with him. I cannot call my gentle, kind and generous maternal grandmother a Baster.

In fact, we should be doing the opposite of continuing to stigmatise – we should de-stigmatise Rehobothers. We have so much work to do in this regard. Already the most prevalent language spoken is Afrikaans, hated for decades as the language of the oppressor. I am happy to find that, at least in the Cape, this stigmatisation is very much on the wane. In fact, it has become quite acceptable not only to speak Afrikaans, but even to incorporate Afrikaans terms like *las* and *bliksem* and *jenne* into English.

Young professional Rehobothers have come a long way to dispel the long-held image of Rehobothers as lacking formal education, being swarthy, and working as builders. The young generation has doctors and journalists, psychologists and engineers. And skin and hair can no longer be used as an indication of ethnic belonging, thanks to modern skin and hair products.

I understand that many Rehobothers use the term "Baster" as a symbol of pride and opposition, if not outright provocation. I can only point out that even Namibians on the whole are totally oblivious of the particular ethnic and historical happenings Rehobothers intend to evoke with the use of this term. Outsiders know and care even less. This attempt falls on deaf ears. We should finally choose how we see ourselves beyond apartheid categories. We should de-colonise our thinking.[62] The rest of the world hardly cares about colour; in effect, we are all of mixed backgrounds.

As a start, why not refer to ourselves as Rehobothers, the people from the town of that name or inhabitants of the Rehoboth Gebiet, in the same way as Londoners hail from London, Parisians are the people who live in Paris, and Berliners are residents of Berlin?

3 LENA OF MY CHILDHOOD

My forefathers unfortunately were not literary people. In fact, some of them were completely illiterate, as was often the case with many mobile, rural families of the day. Keeping diaries, a European tradition, was not part of our lives. Few letters were written or received. Perhaps the German men wrote letters home. More likely they did not. Marrying an indigenous woman was probably nothing to show off about to the relatives in Baden-Württemberg. I imagine my paternal great-grandfather not to have kept his marriage a secret – but I don't know this, as I simply have no evidence. Added to this is the frustrating fact, for me, that my parents never spoke about family history.

When time allowed, I would search for information on family matters in the archives. These were cursory searches, since the focus of my biographical sketches was to be on our kind of life during the apartheid years in rural Namibia and not a family chronicle. Regrettably, my sporadic searches did not end in rich finds. I have bits and pieces that can link events to my family, but little more. However, one such important link follows.

Writing about the history of Rehoboth, Dr. Cornelia Limpricht draws from the diaries of Rhenish missionary Heidmann, who had accompanied the Rehobothers on their trek and subsequently remained their spiritual leader until 1907. Keeping diary fastidiously, he tells how it came to a split within the group during their two-year-long trek. Klaas Swart, head of a small group of families, decided to stay behind at Grootfontein-South, five days' march north of Rehoboth, never joining the Rehoboth group.[63]

True to the tradition of mobility of the day, shortly after the war of 1904, Nikolaas and Marthinus Olivier, accompanied by their sister, Sabina, left the Cape, probably Wellington, and passed through the settlement of Grootfontein-South. The two brothers moved on and eventually applied for citizenship in Rehoboth. Sabina, their sister, stayed behind at Grootfontein-South – for it is here that my paternal great-grandfather, Gustav Dentlinger, must have met and married her.[64] In fact, if her great-grandchild, my aunt Hedi is correct, the exact date was 4 March 1896.[65]

By then the *stigters* (the original settler families of Rehoboth) had been there since 1870. The Oliviers were thus *inkomers* (latecomers) rather than stigters, as were all my Rehoboth relatives. My paternal grandfather Hendrik, obviously of mixed heritage as second-eldest son of Sabina and Gustav, married a woman also of mixed genetic background, Anna Finster. From family accounts I learned that by the mid-1940s, the couple had acquired their farm *Kwartel*, forty-five kilometres west of Rehoboth. A kwartel is a small local bird, and hence a quaint name for a farm.

Hendrik and Anna's second son, Hermann Nikolaas Dentlinger (my father), and Wilhelmine Enssle of mixed heritage (my mother), were married on 25 January 1944 at Rehoboth. While we would sporadically live on one or the other isolated, arid farm in the Rehoboth Gebiet, until my grandfather's death, our home was really on Kwartel. This is where my father and his siblings had grown up.

We lived there spatially separate from my grandparents, Anna Finster and Hennie, as they were known. Their house had a grey dado, roughcast white walls and a corrugated iron pitched roof. A wire fence surrounded the house and yard. Passing through the front garden gate, flanked on either side by a cypress, a straight stone slab walkway led through a symmetrically established garden to the highly polished steps of a cool verandah dotted with wicker chairs and cushions. Notable for the times and the area was that my grandparents' house was compact. [66] Often houses were built in a linear fashion, much like *nagmaal* houses in the Cape: rooms were added one by one, as money allowed. In my grandparents' house, the rooms were interleading, except for the two *stoepkamers*, [67] bedrooms that opened directly onto each end of the verandah. The remaining house had three further rooms: the *voorhuis* (a spacious living room), leading off from that a side bedroom, a kitchen and – also somewhat of an exception for the times – a bathroom.

The colour green comes to mind; light green, glossy oil-painted walls and cool high ceilings and darkness, probably a result of the Prosopis trees blocking the light through the small wooden framed windows. The living room was sparsely furnished with a heavy, dark dining-room table and chairs in the centre and a matching sideboard along the wall. The bedroom had my grandparents' big bed in it and a wardrobe.

The bathroom actually had a ceramic bath, but, inexplicably, no washbasin. Washing of hands was done at the standard – for those days – *wastafel en kroek*, the washstand. The wooden stand was painted white and held an enamel floral basin and the jug filled with water on a lower shelf. The kitchen naturally had a big, homely wood stove, which had to be fed with long-burning acacia logs. A door led out from the kitchen to the backyard and directly in the line of vision beyond the fence was, on the left, the wood pile, source of those wonderful logs, and further to the left still, the outhouse.

One of my most persistent memories is of the ritual connected with using the *kleinhuisie*, the outhouse. You would enter it from the glaring hot sun, close the door behind you and immediately find yourself in complete blackness. After having adjusted to the smell of ammonia and the dark, you would gingerly sit down over the hole in the wooden bench, which made up the long drop. The toilet paper holder was a large nail firmly stuck in the wall at a handy height, its protruding end bent upwards to hold pieces of old newspaper torn into what my grandmother considered to be appropriately sized squares. One would instinctively keep both feet firmly on the ground. The surrounding brick and cement wall of the structure was not solid. Mercifully, through the cracks between the door and its frame or from the ridges of the corrugated iron sheets on the roof, rays of light enabled the eyes to some-what adjust to the dark. However, these spots of light were also entrances for all sorts of insects that would then find a cool, comfortable abode with-in. One did not mind the spiders or even the odd scorpion. It was the fear of the cobra coiled up somewhere in the dark recesses that would keep one alert and the visit short, ready for a hasty retreat.

We occupied our separate, unpainted, very economically designed red brick house some five hundred metres away. My aunts tell me that it was built by my grandfather for my newly married parents. To reach us, one had to cross a shallow gully and then ascend a slight rise to the east of Anna Finster's house. Comprising two rooms, our house was built in a linear fash-ion. One entered a kind of living room and off to the side my parents' bed-room, which we shared. I have no recollection of a kitchen, but am told that there was one off to the back, with a door opening behind the house. If so, then such a kitchen would have had no running water. All water for daily use was carried, bucket by bucket, from the borehole usually in the early morn-ing before the heat of the day. There were no official bathroom facilities as understood in the modern-day sense. To wash the face and hands, we used the usual wooden stand. Mostly, though, we would wash our hands over an enamel pail. When we wanted to have a bath, the *balie* (a big zinc tub) was carried in from outside where it normally doubled as a vessel to hold meat, a tub to hand wash laundry in or any other means of storage. It was placed on the floor and filled with hot water from some or other source. For other purposes, there was always the *veld,* a safe distance from the house. All in all, as a child I had a sense of my grandmother's house being quite elaborate, while ours was quite poor.

We did, however, have a lot of fun on Kwartel. I felt that the relationship between my mother and the female farm employees was exceptional. In those days all employees referred to themselves as being Nama or Damara, the most prevalent indigenous linguistic ethnicities of central Namibia at the time. They spoke Khoe and Afrikaans, but so did all adults in my family. Even until late into my childhood, my parents would often speak Khoe to each other, when they did not want me to understand. I was being taught Khoe by two elderly female employees. They had a lot of fun doing this, for they would send me back and forth between them with messages that had explic-it sexual content, incomprehensible to me, but of great entertainment to them.

All of us, adults and children, would call Lena "Ou Lenas" and Maria "Ou Marias". The form of their names shows how widely various languages had mingled into our everyday speech. *Ou* is Afrikaans for "old", but it is also a term of respect and, I might add, endearment. Whether one spoke German, which my parents only took on suddenly much later, or Afrikaans, one would add the Khoe female suffix "s" to the two women's names, Lena and Maria. So Ou Lenas and Ou Marias is what they remained until this day.

The two women were actually employed by my grandmother, Anna Finster. However, on the odd occasion, they would come separately or together to see whether they could help with the work at our little red brick house. I use the word "help" in the broadest sense, as I can only remember ever seeing my mother work. They would come walking majestically towards us with their voluminous dresses gracefully swaying with each step. Once arrived, they would sit down like plump hens in front of the kitchen area. There they would each be offered tea in huge enamel cups, reserved specifically for their use. Only once they had savoured their tea, sucking it in by hollowing their cheeks and flicking the dregs of the leaves from the cup onto the ground, did anything actually happen. They would try not to budge from the spot they had found, all the while chatting to my mother while she worked. Often she would be hand-washing the laundry in flat, white enamel basins. Then, with strong arms, she would wring the water out of the sheets by forming them into long twisted bands of wet fabric. Ou Lenas might lend a hand by leaning forward from her sitting position, grabbing the end of the sheet to stop it from falling onto the sand or back into the water. Apart from her hands reaching forward, the bottom part of her body would remain firmly rooted to the spot. My mother would be in constant motion, wringing and rinsing.

Ou Lenas, my
son Stephan
and myself at
Tierkolkies, 1994

Ou Lenas at Tierkolkies, 1994

Mostly these visits were social events. Ou Lenas and Ou Marias were big chatters and storytellers. I remember vividly how a certain regular occurrence brought Khoe mythology to life for me. All of us on the farm had occasionally noticed a strange light shining in my parents' bedroom window at night. Ou Lenas had obviously also seen it, because her conical traditional Khoe hut (called *a pondok* in my youth) directly faced our house. I remember the discussion of this strange phenomenon the next day. She suggested that it was the giant serpent with the diamond on its head, that shone so brightly that it could be seen so far and so distinctly. Much later as a young anthropology student, I read about this Khoe myth. At some point, I realised that it simply was the light of the moon shining onto the window pane of my parents' bedroom. Perhaps this story, too, was for my benefit, as were others like the one that told of children actually being baby baboons that had their tails cut off.

I truly loved the two women, in spite of them having been big teasers, with me often being at the mercy of their jokes. They were also smart. They interacted with us casually and confidently. Yet, already to a child's eye, I could notice odd distances being imposed and maintained. One was the differently reserved drinking utensils. Another was an unspoken physical distance. I picked up the subtle clues and acted accordingly. For instance, once the two of them had installed themselves outside our kitchen, I would join them and sit on their laps in turn. However, before I actually did so, I would fetch a towel or a dishcloth, drape it over the lap of either woman (my choice for the day) and then sit down on that. This had many undertones. They would turn this childish slight into a standard joke. The minute I arrived, I would be told: "Go and fetch your clean towel and come and sit on my lap, my child." I remember my mother neither rebuking nor correcting them in any of their games or their sympathetic revenge, as one might have expect-ed of an employer. She might half-heartedly have said: "Now, why must you carry on teasing the child like this?" but would laugh along with them. Presumably I believed their clothes to be soiled by the cooking fire, the work among the sheep or the milking of the goats. Consequently, perhaps because of my mother's youth in the presence of these older women, this banter between them and me seemingly was allowed to pursue its own natural course. Perhaps she was unsure of how to deal with the situation. It did not dampen our spirits, even though the whole exercise was repeated each time they visited. They probably considered their visits as a form of entertain-ment sought and enjoyed by both parties, in a hot and desolate environment with a monotonous lifestyle mostly boring to all.

My family had left the Gebiet in 1963. Even though we now lived in the white area of Namibia, I felt drawn back to Rehoboth and the family farms. I would visit whenever I had a chance, mostly with my late mother, whose rel-atives had all remained there. It was during those years as a student work-ing in the Namib Desert, that I started going back to *Tierkolkies* ("tiger spots"), the farm of my paternal uncle adjacent to and east of Kwartel.

Tierkolkies is situated thirty-eight kilometres from Rehoboth. On these occasions I would see my favourite uncle, but also Ou Lenas. She had in the meantime left Kwartel to live and work here instead. We would sit under the old blue gum trees outside the farmhouse and talk, all of us. Then in 1984, I married, and my husband and I left for the United States. It would be years before I would return. When I finally did so, the occasion had a special mean-ing for both Ou Lenas and me.

In the summer of 1993, after almost a decade of absence and with a new approach to my mixed ancestry, I once again found myself sitting outside the kitchen under the old blue gum trees of the Tierkolkies farmhouse. My uncle had since lost his battle with cancer. But the blue gums had persevered and so had my beloved childhood *aia*, support, healer, substitute mother.

As she came walking down the well-trodden path from her own house some two hundred metres away, it seemed no different from all the other times before. Actually I need not even have watched her. I could close my eyes and still see her wind her way around the chicken and goose pens. They started cackling and hissing at her. She shooed them off by pointing at them with her walking stick: *"Etse !gu. Ei, ne ghoen na!"* – "Go away! Oh, these things!" she said in Khoe. Coming closer I could see her from the side now. Her voluminous, ground-length dress still swayed with her movements as it had during my childhood. Then she was in front of me. Close up, her face remained ageless, the same expression of wistfulness around her eyes, the pointed moles on her pitch-black nose. But it also became immediately evident to me that the rest of her had aged. Ou Lenas of my childhood now leaned more heavily on her cane, she walked somewhat slower, her shoulders more stooped than in my memory. Still after all this time, her face had not changed. I had to control my emotions, so touched was I to be with her again.

"How aaaare you?" She characteristically lengthened the vowels. "Noooo, I was wondering whether you would ever come back again, my child. But now I am satisfied, that I see you here." By now I was forty-two years old, but her loving greeting had not changed.

She, too, was touched, but quickly got control of her feelings, as she waited for me to answer. A swift rundown of my ten years of married life in the United States, and of being a mother of two lively boys brought us smoothly to the subject of her health. Her eyes were her biggest problem. She was virtually blind in the left eye, she told me. I saw the milky whiteness of the iris and immediately thought of cataracts. She continued to offer a tale of numerous trips to the hospital in Rehoboth, back and forth, their diagnosis not really satisfying her.

"And then there is the rheumatism. Do you know what that feels like? It hurts so much. One does not really feel like doing anything, but just sitting and doing nothing. For this, too, I have been to hospital, in fact in Windhoek. They gave me some tablets, which really helped, but I have run out of them now. They weren't prepared to give me more and, of course, one cannot run there every few minutes. In the olden days, one would just *smeer* – we would massage these pains away."

"What did you use to massage with?" I asked, trying to get back some semblance of control of the situation.

"Oh, simply *met die vet* – with some lard," she replied.

I was once again reminded of the ingenuity of rural people when they come to deal with the trying conditions of life.

I battled somewhat to turn the conversation towards my intention to do a more formal interview this time; perhaps I could publish her life story – but she pressed on: "I have heard on the radio of interviews just like this one, and people usually start by asking the other person their age," she reminded me. Nine years of my anthropological training were mercilessly made obsolete as she took over the interview. "There I won´t be able to help you at all. My *kop-kaart* – identity document – is with one of the children. Anyway, it's not worth anything, because when the DTA[68] came in, they gave people these and put any information on them, just to get them to vote for their party."

So, my aunt, standing by on the side and my cousin were summoned to help with the calculations of the date of her birth. We started, as is usual in rural parts of Namibia, with the big rains of 1930 or 1933, working our way backwards until we came to the general estimate of somewhere around 1905. This made her just over ninety years old! She found no fault with that. Then we continued.

"Well, how are your children?" I asked, knowing that this was always a fruitful subject. There was no need to prompt.

"Saros, my last daughter now lives in Rehoboth," she answered readily.

"Now is she a child of Danster, your late husband?" I needed the details and confirmation after all these years.

"Yes, all my eleven children are from Danster," she answered smoothly.

This was hard to believe. In rural as well as urban Namibia, serial monogamous relationships are the norm – sequential but often long-term relationships with a number of men – and thus diverse parenthood. I decided to leave it at that, suspecting she intended to present an image of herself as she wanted me to see her. Instead I asked her to please repeat this for the record: "How did you meet Danster?" The following repetition of one of my favourite childhood tales was not disappointing.

"I met him at !Khubus [Kobos, a mine south-west of Rehoboth] where I grew up. Danster had come from the south of the country. At the time I was working for an Afrikaans family who owned the mine shop at !Khubus. Danster was employed at the mine. Every day the men would pass the yard of the house adjacent to the mine shop where I worked.

" 'Good morning, afternoon!' they would call. 'How are you, woman?' some would ask. We would always chat. That is *waar ons gekry het mekaar* – where we found each other.

"One day he asked me, 'Where do you live?'

" 'I live right over there,' I said, pointing to my room that stood close by the house of my employer.

" 'I want to come and visit you,' he said to me, forthright. And he came; and that very first day he came to visit me, he said: 'I want you to know that my visiting you here, *nou dat jy my ontvang het* – now that you have received me, *dis nie vir die kombers nie* – it is not for the blanket.' And he continued: 'So, you must go and tell your *grootmense* – old people – that I am coming to see them *vir die trou* – for marriage.'

"So, I went to my employer and told him that there was this short man who was after me, saying I should inform my family that he would come and see them for marriage. He is not interested in the blanket. And I was thinking of taking some time off to make preparations to see whether he would actually come to visit on Saturday, as he said he would. I left for my parents' house, which was a little distance away, and told them of this wooing going on."

I commented on the direct but honest and friendly manner in which he had initiated the conversation; there was certainly no beating around the bush.

"Yes," she remembered, "he was not a man to twist his words or *wat draaie geloop het nie* – who walked in curves."

"And he was not shy either, was he then?" I wanted to pursue the subject.

"*Oooohh nooo*," she said. "*Hy't sy sê gesê* – he would say his say. I arrived at my parents' house and told them; and they said: '*Nouja*, let us see this man. Let him come.' That was what they said." Both hands were flying to her side to emphasise her point.

"There was no problem?" I prompted.

"No, there is no problem with a child that wants to marry according to the proper and legal manner." She raised her voice to stress how easy and logical this was. "So, truly there he comes on Saturday afternoon and sits and talks and talks ... and then he asks quite freely: '*Hierdie kom wat ek gekom het, my ma en pa, het ek gekom vir daardie vrou*' – this coming of mine is for this woman, my father and mother.

" 'Yes, she told us that you were coming for marriage and nothing else; and now we have seen you. And we also do not want the blanket, as you yourself say. So, there is no problem.' "

We are both speechless once again, at the direct manner of Danster's request and his frank behaviour as well as the obvious logic of the custom.

"Everybody seemed happy," I finally managed to say. "Then the next step?" This was my favourite part of the story.

"Well, now everything was *oopgepraat* – open and clear. So, he would come to my house at work and talk, and visit and woo me. Now everything was free. And then one day, he came and asked me when I was going home again. I told him. In the meantime, he had asked two of his older people to stand in for his parents, who were too far away. When next I arrived home, these two older folk were already there, talking with my parents' people the same language of wedding negotiations.

It did not take him more than twelve months and he had saved together the money, of which he gave a share to my employer for a wedding dress. So, my employer's daughter, who was a wonderful seamstress, sewed me a white wedding dress. It was beautiful! They even bought me a pair of white *tekkies* – pumps – and stockings and white *handskoene* – gloves. My husband wore a black suit, white shirt and jacket, maybe brown shoes. Today they marry in

Missionary
Vollmer and
Pastor Jakobus
Beukes in
Rehoboth, ca
1955. ELCRN
Archives

light-coloured suits, but in those days we wore dark suits. With a jacket and all. And I and my brother, we were both married on the same day in the Rhenish Church in Rehoboth by missionary Vollmer."

"So, you were both married in Rehoboth?" This and the following I remembered well from my childhood.

"We went back to !Khubus, made the wedding there. Those days people did not take *kikkiese en goed* - photographs and things. *Ek het skaap geslag* - I slaughtered a sheep. *Die wat bok geslag het, het bok geslag* - those who wanted to slaughter a goat, slaughtered a goat. Danster slaughtered two sheep and my brother slaughtered a young heifer, not much bigger than that sheep over there."

This comment was followed by laughter, with head thrown back, white teeth showing. The humour was on account of her brother not having been rich; the heifer he slaughtered was only the size of a sheep.

"So, you really loved him, did you not?" This was stating the obvious, I thought, but I would be surprised.

"Hmmmm, I was so much in love with him. I got so many children from him. Let me count them for you. Saros, Johanna, Jan, Magriet, Damasol, Ganab, Gheibie, Faleen, Hakhas, Hokhans, Viool ... eleven children in all I got from him; him alone. No other man. Seven sons and five daughters."

Here she held up her left hand, counting off the numbers with her right index finger. Her calculation was wrong here. Perhaps one child had died. However I was to find out later that actually Jan, her first son, was from another man. Instead, I continued: "How many years were you married for?" She laughed, with a little sideways look to my aunt. I scolded myself secretly for assuming she thought about time in terms of years. Did I embarrass her?

"I cannot say. I did not count. Many years with all those many children ..."

I tried a different approach: "Did he love you?"

"Yes. When I got married my parents said to me: 'My child, today you take this man who has taken you in marriage. Our love now passes on from us to him. He will now take care of you, as we have taken care of you. Today you take him as a father and you take him as a mother.' "

I wanted to know how she assessed his feelings towards her. "Was he good to you?"

"He was good to me. He was good. You see those days were easier than today. Things were not expensive. It was the days of *tikkies,* sixpence and shillings.[69] A reel of thread could be bought for a *tikkie;* two shillings and a sixpence would buy you a whole dress, five or six yards of cloth. We did not know hunger or poverty. It was during this easy time *dat ek die ou getrou het* – that I married the man. We did not lack anything."

Obviously, she had needed to warm up to what was coming. Had she been presenting the ideal picture to me rather than the real one?

"Later, he would start hitting, but *ek het uitgehou* – I persevered. He would hit, particularly during the later few years he would hit a lot, - *maar ek het uitgehou.*"

I was shocked. I had not heard this before. Had she kept it from me all these years, possibly because she thought I was too young to hear of such matters? "When did this start?" I needed to know.

"Perhaps after we were married three or four years. *Toe is die ou sommer opstandelik* – suddenly he became aggressive. I could not say a thing before he would become upset. One could not discuss anything and one would no longer *hoormekaar* – hear each other, agree with each other. I would leave it then until later. It would just end in fighting. And so we remained."

"So did he hit with the hand?" This had never been part of the story that I had loved so much.

"With the hand? *Aaaiii,* with sticks and anything he could lay his hands on - *kirriese en goed*. There are many Khoe men who will hit with a whip or will take off their belts to hit you with. Normally they will hurt you with anything they can find."

I was getting upset and incredibly sad. "But still you stayed together? For so long?" This new information was becoming increasingly worrying to me.

"Yes, that is why people would say: 'This couple fights so much, but then we see that she is pregnant again and that the child is born. And the woman does not look too unhappy or dissatisfied, she is staying.'

"And I would say: 'Well, I swore that I would stay with him until death.'"

"And so you remained at !Khubus?" I asked, wondering why she did not leave.

"We stayed in !Khubus for another few years. Then the shop closed, and for a while we worked for my old employer on one of his farms, herding sheep, then for another Baster farmer in the area. But because he wanted to move away from the region and we preferred to stay, we found ourselves work on Kwartel. My older sister already worked for old Anna and Hennie. Do you remember old Anna? She called herself Anna Finster and not Dentlinger? She was such a proud woman that she would call herself by her own name and not that of her married husband. And your grandfather, Hennie Dentlinger? Do you remember him?

"We knew all the farms of the area from driving past them with our donkey carts on our way to and from Rehoboth. So, Danster got work on Kwartel with your grandparents. First as a tamer of their racehorses, tamed them, tamed them, tamed them … and then later as 'n veewagter - a stock herder - and so we stayed on."

Following this, our conversation turned to more pleasant matters. I asked her: "When you came to Kwartel, did you already have any of your children?"

"Yes, I had Johanna and I had Jan. Jan was here yesterday. He slaughtered a lamb. I told him that you were coming. He lives in a big house in Rehoboth," she told me.

"In those days did you go to hospital to deliver your children?" I wanted to know.

"No, nie een van my kinders - not one of my eleven children - was born in the hospital. I gave birth to the first two at my mother's house; two more were born on Kwartel. Then I moved to this farm, Tierkolkies. For the first one I conceived here, I went back to my mother's to have it there.

"After that birth my mother said to me: 'This is the third and last child I will catch for a married daughter of mine - a daughter who has a husband. When another child now arrives, you tell your husband to find an elderly woman who will look after you. If you need to be massaged, she should do so; when the child arrives, she should catch it and cut the umbilical cord. You must learn by yourself, how to give birth to the children. How the pains come, you must learn yourself. And if you are alone, you must teach your husband how to help you at the birth, how he must support from the back, how he must cut the umbilical cord.' So I delivered three of my children, Hokhans, Kheibie and Damasol all by myself with Danster on Kwartel."

Having recently given birth myself, I compared her version to the one I knew from the States: prenatal classes and then constant medical attention. I was amazed at how she could accept her situation as totally normal. After finding my speech again, I asked her, "Now, what is object of the massaging?"

"Well, sometimes during a pregnancy the foetus is not positioned right, it lies across the stomach, the head is in the hip. For these kinds of things you massage. The head must face down. You feel whether the head is positioned correctly. If it is not, you have to turn it.[70] If it is lying on its back, you have to turn it. If you as a mother lie on your back a lot, it also will turn onto its back. This is bad. You will have to position it correctly. The feet and the arms, too, must point downwards. It cannot be pointing outwards."

She was obviously describing a breech birth and how to prevent this by massaging. I was keen to learn more and wanted to know: "But this must be hard to turn the foetus around?"

She was just as clear on this matter as my gynaecologist back home. "Yes, it is very hard work. You cannot turn it in one go. You keep trying. Then the woman must remain bed-ridden in the same position, so that the foetus does not jump back into its old position again. You keep doing this, until all is right. You skip a few days, because her body will hurt from the massaging. Then you try again after a few days. Another serious problem occurs when the umbilical cord is twisted around the neck of the child."

I was intrigued and not quite convinced. "Well, that must be very hard to feel. What do you do in that case?"

"Yes, it is hard to feel. But before the birth you can detect it with massaging, then you know, that at birth you must be extremely careful and quick. In a case like that, when the birth process starts, your hands must already be there to loosen the cord, just as I am loosening the string of these beads."

She let the beads on a string around her neck glide over her hands, guiding them in a specific direction. I could not help thinking of the many years modern gynaecologists were forced to study until receiving their degrees. "I suppose not every woman is cut out for this kind of work. Does one learn it?"

"No, not every woman can do this. You have to learn it. My mother taught me. Whenever she had to go and treat a pregnant woman with problems, she would take me with her and ask me to help her. She would say: 'Massage here' and I would do it, while she would massage and press on another spot. 'Push here and then press there!' And I would do it. In this way I practised a long time. You must do it like this. Press here. Massage there. This is how I learned."

I was thinking of all the other women, who bore children in my childhood and who had all lived in the area. I asked, "Did you then help a lot of women in this way?"

There was no hesitation in her answer. "Terribly, terribly, terribly many. We were three women on Kwartel, all old Hennie's employees. There was old cripple Marias - do you remember Ou Marias?"

Did I remember her? Ou Marias helped raise my sister and me. "You would always send me back and forth between the two of you with messages to be passed on in Khoe, and even though you had taught me Khoe quite well, I did not know all the terms you used. You would make them embarrassing messages. How could I ever forget Ou Marias?"

This elicited piercing peals of laughter, which went on for quite a while.

"I would tell you in Khoe to say to Ou Marias: 'Lenas says I should tell you to send your *!urus* – vagina – with me to give to her.' At Maria's house you would repeat this. She, in turn, would send you back with the message: 'I cannot send my vagina, please you send yours!' When you then arrived at my house, you would repeat Marias's instruction in beautiful Khoe: *'Sa !urusa uha ta ma ha* – I did not bring her vagina with me. Please send yours.' In this way we would send you back and forth with these messages. *Ons het ons doodgelag* – we killed ourselves laughing! Your mother would laugh and say, 'Now why do you tease her so much with these messages?' And we would say to her, 'It's a language she must learn to speak.' "

After howls of laughter and much clapping of hands and slapping of thighs, she finally composed herself and continued: "So, Ou Marias and I, and Ou Marthas on Kwartel, we would always play midwives to all the mothers. For example, if !Xhoras had conceived and was close to giving birth, Marthas and I would massage her. And if I was pregnant, they would massage me and deliver my baby. And again, if Marthas was pregnant, we would help her. And there was not one problem with all these children. They all grew up to become healthy adults.

"One herb we frequently used was Khoxab. It is a bush. It grows on this farm as well. One of us would go and dig it up. This would clean the uterus. Sometimes the moeder – the afterbirth – stays inside you for three or four days."

"How does one use this medication?" I wanted to know.

Still speaking as the knowledgeable midwife and healer, she tells me: "You brew a tea out of it and drink it and it will clean the uterus completely. You will have no further problems."

"And when you cut the cord what did you do?" I thought we might as well cover all the topics of childbirth.

"We would cut it and put a gauze around the base of it on the baby's stomach. Sometimes we would tie it down with another gauze around the baby's stomach, so that it does not dry out. The wound we would treat with Black Balsam and cover it again until it has healed."

"And then did you watch out for the afterbirth?"

"Yes, that would come out later," she continued, obviously an expert in midwifery matters.

"Did you do anything with it?"

"We would bury it together with the dirty water and the water we had used for washing. You cannot cut the umbilical cord, until the afterbirth has come down. If you do, the cord will jump back into the uterus and the mother will die. If this happens we would tie the end of the cord to the thigh of the mother. The mother would then have to feel for herself and wait for the post-birth pains, which bring down the afterbirth. You see, the birth of the child is not as serious as the coming down of the afterbirth. It is wonderful how it comes down and then, of course, the uterus stays behind for the next foetus. It is a miracle how the Lord has made this to function."

To her it was all perfectly clear and logical. I was slightly sceptical, but let it go. Perhaps certain points were lost in the translation between Khoe and Afrikaans. "You must have had your children one after the other? And you were being looked after by your friends?"

"I never had any problems conceiving and giving birth," she said with enjoyment. "And with me it worked so well that after a day or two, I would go back to work. I would nurse them for six months or so. When they were very young, I would take them with me to work tied on my back. I would stop in-between and nurse them. Or I would lay them down on the floor and let them sleep there. I always had enough milk as well. At a later age I would leave them with an older child to look after, while I was at work. After four months, they would get *pap* or *dikmelk* – porridge or sour milk. Thank goodness I never had any problems."

"It sounds as if this arrangement worked very well between you women. But was it also like that in your work?" I was curious to know whether she also saw it in this way, and was surprised by her politically conventional answer.

"We had no problems. The things worked very well, not like now. An employer was a *baas*, an employee was a *booi*. The employer would respect the employee and the employee would respect the employer."

After this first lengthy conversation, I visited Ou Lenas whenever I was in Namibia. Each time I saw her, I would think that this surely must be the last time, but I would see her at least five more times. Once in 2006 we met in Rehoboth at a funeral; she was burying her son, Jan, who had died of a heart attack. She had received new spectacles which she was wearing proudly, even though they fitted badly. She had in the meantime had a cataract operation, miraculously regaining her eyesight after three or four years of almost complete blindness. This condition she had mentioned during our first reunion. However, she was not in a mood for conversation on the day of the funeral. So I heard the details about the operation from my cousin, Harold.

"The operation was done in Windhoek. Apparently when she was able to open her eyes afterwards in the ward, she only dimly saw the shapes of the medical staff. She quickly closed her eyes again, not believing that this was real. When she dared open them again, she looked at her hands, turning them before her eyes, turning them over and over in wonder. She had not been able to see them for years. She marvelled at them. However, the true realisation only hit home when she was discharged from hospital and rode by bus from Windhoek to Rehoboth. Apparently she never stopped talking during the bus trip, explaining to everyone about the farms and the surroundings.

"In Rehoboth she was picked up by my mother. Lenas could not believe that she was seeing the mountains and the farms once again. However the highlight was here, right here on the farm. I arrived some time after she had moved back into her own house. I sent a message up to her house with one of the children, asking her please to come down to the farmhouse. I wanted to know for myself whether she could see again.

"I was watching her from the kitchen, where I sat, observing how she came walking down the path. As always she was talking to herself as she walked, commenting this time on things she could see again. As she came closer to the kitchen, she stopped in the doorway, looking at me. Of course, she hadn't been able to see me during her blindness. Still leaning with one hand on her walking-stick, the other above her against the doorframe, she asked: 'And when did you turn so grey?' "

We both laughed, shook our heads knowingly, marvelling at the humour Ou Lenas would come up with, even in the most unsuspecting moments. How free she felt in saying her say, in just the very manner it occurred to her – not disrespectful, but forthright.

The next time I saw her, she must have been more than a hundred years old, according to our initial calculation. She no longer could walk down the well-trodden path. I now had to walk past the blue gums and then past the fowl pen and up to her house. Her spirit and humour were still evident. In the same manner as she greeted my cousin, she commented on my appearance (characteristically putting the tops of her fingers to her lips, turning her head and looking into the distance): *"Hocha, ti Elob Ao* – dear God, you have really grown fat." And at my following visit, she would comment: "Last time the hair was light, now it is dark."

This time we talked at great length about the loss of all her many children. Shortly after she had buried Jan, her last daughter had died. She was truly moved by the fact that she, their mother, had outlived them all. *"Dis mos nie reg nie* – it is not right. A parent should go before her children."

Since the previous meeting in 2006, whenever I would see her, a man called Johannes was never far from her side. An air of togetherness exuded from them. In 2006 she had casually introduced him to me. When I finally realised that they were a pair, I asked her how and when he had come into her life. She was not going to give anything away.

"Hy was mos nog altyd daar - he has always been with me."

Here my cousin cut in, saying that Johannes was the reason Danster would hit her so much. *"Julle twee het gevry mekaar onder sy neus* - the two of you were courting each other right under his nose."

Johannes just laughed. I looked at his wrinkled, good-natured face under the broad-brimmed hat and wondered whether that was the reason for his broken nose. I asked him, "How did you break your nose? Was it Danster who hit you?"

"No, this happened when I was a young child. My aunt hit me with an iron pipe."

I did not want to waste this rare opportunity of being able to talk to him and expressed my sympathy in a deep sigh, but silently was shocked by the extent of violence already mentioned by Ou Lenas.

"So, did Danster ever hit you, as they all tell me he did?"

"Yes, he did hit me. Once he came at me with the lid of an iron pot. While I was standing at the fire not expecting anything, he hit me with that lid. Here, right here on the side of my neck under my head." He indicated with his straight hand just under the ear. *"Ek het daar geval* - I fell to the side. After I came to, I said to all standing around me: 'Now I will take his wife!'"

I was surprised by the determination in the voice of this normally peaceful man, and by the nature of his revenge. Quite evidently this determination shown many decades ago has persevered until this day.

In February 2009 I saw Ou Lenas and her Johannes once again. I drove from Rehoboth to the farm, taking with her grandson, Hendrik, the son of Jan. During the drive there, we were chatting happily. He talked of Jan, his father and his death from a stroke in 2006, how he had had high blood pressure. How he was looking forward to visiting Ou Lenas, his grandmother, and how they had arranged a party for her one-hundred-and-sixth birthday some time back. When we arrived at Tierkolkies, we were soon surrounded by more of her grandchildren and great-grandchildren.

When my cousin finally did bring her by car to come to the main farmhouse, it was quite evident that she was very sick and weak from some form of stomach flu. In spite of this, numerous great-grandchildren came with her and supported her where they could. Valencia, Harold's wife, immediately administered medication and cooked a watery broth for both old people. Ou Lenas tried, but she was too weak to even talk. Johannes, always at her side, volunteered that truly this was the last time we would sit and talk.

"But now we are getting old. We will not live much longer. *Die liggaam is moeg* - there is a tiredness in our bodies. We feel a tiredness that does not want to leave us ..."

I remember being struck by his continuous use of the pronoun "we". I envied them for their feeling of belonging together.

During my visit to them in 2010, I gave Johannes some money and said, "You need to have money in case anything happens to Ou Lenas. Take this money, split it and hide it." Two weeks after my visit to them when I was once again in Europe, a phone call informed me that Johannes had passed away. This was truly a shock to me. Everybody had obviously assumed that she would be the first to go.

During my two visits in 2011, I found her in Rehoboth living with one of her daughters-in-law. I was upset by the poor living arrangements. The corrugated iron room must have been cold in winter, hot in summer. However, it seemed to be her choice to be there. Another aunt and I arranged to have food sent to her on a regular basis. Other relatives of the family also brought her food. In spite of her aches and pains of old age that she complained about to us, she still enjoyed a good joke and remembered the old times.

In July 2012, a week before I was to arrive in Namibia, I got the message that she had passed away. She had died peacefully on 9 July. This was twenty-two days before her one-hundred-and-seventh birthday. On the day of the funeral, the Lutheran Church in Block E of Rehoboth was packed. Young people were standing in the aisles. Her family gave her an elaborate funeral with no expense spared.

I felt very fortunate to have been able to lay to rest the woman who had been part of our family for more than eighty years. She was one of the most psychologically grounded people I have come across. She was smart, but loving and forgiving. She was quite aware of her status as a matriarch in her own family and her value as a person in the area. She was the communal midwife, doctor and healer. All and sundry came to her for treatment, including my mother during her pregnancy. In the end she was surrounded by numerous grandchildren and great-grandchildren. She was fearless. By rights she was an employee, but was never treated as one, nor did she act as one. She was simply part of our lives, as an equal in her own right. She was wise. What could she have done once her husband became abusive? Leave the farm? Have him leave? Would this have been possible in those days? Instead, she quietly, but deliberately started an affair with a more gentle, more understanding partner, Johannes - a relationship that would last until the end of his life.

Since ethnicity has played a major role in my own life, I admire the manner in which she totally ignored it. She was as black as the ace of spades.[71] However, in all the talks we had, Ou Lenas never once made any mention of prejudice towards her on the basis of genetics or ethnicity. I would like to believe that on the farm, we actually defied apartheid in many ways.

If we believe psychologists to be correct in saying that the early few years of life are the most formative, then she certainly contributed immensely to shaping my personality. As must be the case for many people of southern Africa who have been raised by indigenous employees, she must have been the initiator of a large part of my personal value system. I hope that she transmitted to me some of her tenacity, humour, confidence, generosity, freedom of spirit yet humility, some of her compassion, tolerance and wisdom. Above all, I know she contributed to my realisation that ethnicity should set no boundaries.

Sadly, as time went on we would not be able to continue ignoring ethnicity as we had done on the farm. For some of us, ethnicity and genetics would come to play a major role in our lives.

4 HEDI'S STORY

> Of all the things that happened during those years, I remember the trial in Karibib the best. It was the end of our flight from the police. Actually, it was the end of a lot of problems and struggles.

This is how Hedi, my aunt, started re-telling those partly humorous, but mostly painful events of her youth in the late forties and beginning of the fifties. She was searching for the right words. She spoke a Namibian kind of German, not the language she had grown up with, stumbling over ideas, sometimes haltingly, a little anxiously. Now and then emotions would get the better of her as she tried to recall how the unbelievable had happened.

We were sitting on the walled verandah of her spacious older home in Windhoek. Around us stood several potted plants as tall as we were, sheltering us from perhaps more than the heat outside. She was relating the frustrating circumstances of her premarital years. I had first heard her story when I was a student, decades ago. Because of my own situation then, I had listened hesitantly, yet intrigued. Listening to it this time was different. With apartheid dismantled, I felt a wonderful freedom to now be able to talk about our past openly. She saw this differently. More than anything, she was proud of what she had achieved, but was not yet ready to come out whole-

Hedi mid 1950s

heartedly and admit her heritage. She still feared repercussions for her grandchildren. Even so, we had agreed to record the events of her life. We were unsure what we would do with them, but simply felt her story needed to be told.

> At the trial, I remember all of us sitting in a small narrow room in the magistrate's court, on some worn wooden benches facing a podium. We had to wait patiently a long time, for the magistrate took his time to come. On the other side of the aisle sat Hans, the man who was going to be my husband. He was already wearing those heavy glasses. Do you remember how he had always suffered from bad eyesight … ever since he was young?

She smiled at me somewhat hesitantly, waiting for me to confirm that this was how I also remembered him. "Of course, he always looked dusty and oil-stained from the work he did on the cars," I said, referring to the automobiles he was constantly fixing in his backyard and reselling. "And his thick-lensed glasses were always smudged." Satisfied, she collected her thoughts again and continued:

> On my right sat my father, Hennie. Next to him sat, Hermann, your father. Yes, your father was there.

I had forgotten that detail and looked at her surprised. She nodded at me seriously. I noticed that her previously dark brown hair was now grey, swept up and held in a clasp at the top of her head.

> At the end of the bench sat our attorney, van der Maade. He had come sixty kilometres from Omaruru to Karibib to represent us at the trial. I no longer remember every detail – it was a long time ago – but I think he was recommended to Hans by a friend. The two of them must have made contact after our arrests.
>
> Hans had made all the arrangements and then finally van der Maade had let us know about the date of the trial. Then the morning before the trial he wanted to see both of us. When I finally met him, I remember being somewhat surprised. He didn't ask many questions at all during that meeting. It was almost like an omen.
>
> All this time Hans had continued staying at Karibib, living in the little room at the hotel we had previously occupied together. Obviously, I couldn't stay there with him. My father, your father and I had driven all the way from Kwartel to Karibib the previous day to get to the trial. So, our little group of three was forced to camp in the open at a spot near the edge of town

under some trees. When van der Maade then wanted to meet with us, he
was able to arrange for a table to be put in the verandah area of the hotel.
Then I could actually physically be there too.

These exceptional arrangements were quite the order of the day. After all,
this was 1955, already the height of the apartheid era.[72] After World War II,
Namibia effectively became part of South Africa. Thus, when the National
Party won the South African elections in 1948, its now official apartheid pol-
icies of racial segregation were imposed on Namibia.

The laws of racial segregation were complex and contradictory, sometimes arbitrarily interpreted, as we shall see. For instance, the Separate
Amenities Act of 1953 stipulated that certain public places such as hotels,
were to be frequented only by individuals belonging to the "white race". Van
der Maade, the attorney acting for Hedi and Hans, was such a person
declared white, whereas Hedi, her brother Hermann and her father Hendrik,
were not permitted into the hotel as they came from Rehoboth, an area
reserved for people of mixed or coloured heritage.

Therefore on this decisive day of their lives, sitting inside the magistrate's court, the three of them looked somewhat dishevelled. The men
had not shaved, nor had there been a possibility to wash. Hedi remembered
that

we had all slept in various positions of discomfort in our old grey Ford
under some sparsely leafed acacia trees at the edge of town.

The purpose of the trial was to pronounce a verdict on at least two, if not
three contraventions of the law by Hedi and her Hans. Apartheid laws were
designed to keep the races[73] separate. Hence, the two were doomed from the
moment they fell in love. Hedi, "coloured" from the law's point of view, was
having an affair with Hans, legally "white" from Swakopmund, a white town
per apartheid definition. They had been living together. This was a contravention of yet another proclamation, which forbade people of different races
to live in the areas reserved for white people only. Secondly, they were
involved in an extramarital sexual relationship with each other, which was
prohibited between individuals of different races. Of course they could not
marry, because that was forbidden by virtue of the prohibition of mixed marriages. It was for these reasons that they had been arrested and now had to
stand trial in Karibib.[74] Under such convoluted legal circumstances, one can
only be grateful that sanity prevailed. For Hedi recalls:

Actually, the night before the trial, we did not worry much about what was
going to happen the next day. By then we had been separated for many

weeks. Everyone's advice after our arrests, had been that we should remain apart and not be seen together for a while, since this might increase our chances of a positive verdict. So, Hans had remained in Karibib and I had stayed on the farm with my parents. That night at last we had the opportunity of a few private moments together. Hans had sneaked out of town to come and see us. We were so excited to be together again. We were young and in love and were simply happy to be in each other's company. Afterwards he had to return to our little room in the hotel, where we had lived for two months and where, legally, I was not allowed to be ...

She sighed, leaning back in her chair, reminiscing. Eventually she continued, talking of the trial the next day.

Finally the magistrate entered the room. We all rose. I must admit, I felt as if detached from reality, as if all of this was happening to somebody else. Many thoughts were racing through my mind.

She must have wondered why on earth she was there. Her anger must have risen. For the millionth time she must have felt the humiliating unfairness of being judged, not only by laws that were imposed by a government occupying her country as a mandate, but - injury upon injury - by laws that the majority of local inhabitants had not voted for.[75] She was an innocent victim of history. Why should she be judged for the consequences of historical processes that she had taken no part in, according to decisions made by people unknown to her in a part of the world she had never seen? And now here she stood, treated like a common criminal for having contravened these laws; she was truly caught in the web of historical forces beyond her control.

After all we had worked for to shape our lives the way we wanted to live them, will the law now permit me to continue doing so with Hans by my side? Or will I be forced to return to my previous life? But there was nothing I could do until the verdict. I felt paralysed.

Yet before I could come back to earth, everything was over. "Your Honour, would you, classify this lady as coloured or as white?" van der Maade had asked the magistrate.

With the magistrate's answer, the trial was over. All the agony of the previous months, the fear and the harassment by the police was over. We walked out in a daze. This was the confusing paradox, the happy climax of my life ... but my story actually starts long before this. Its beginning is really the same as the beginning of Namibia as we know it today. It goes back to when the first Germans arrived in the country.

In the early 1880s, Adolf Lüderitz, a German trader, began to buy huge tracts of land[76] on the coast of Namibia.[77] With the encouragement of the German government he soon owned almost the entire coast stretching approximately one hundred and fifty kilometres inland. As a result, the formerly indecisive Bismarck now became more directly involved in the process of settlement of the last available region of Africa, albeit a rather desolate one. In the wake of these international developments, Hedi's grandfather – my great-grandfather, Gustav Dentlinger – became caught up in this new political activity of German expansion in Africa.

> My grandfather left his native Irslingen, just north of Rottweil at the eastern edge of the Schwarzwald in Württemberg, and in 1892 together with two friends (a Herr Hummel and a Herr Pegel), boarded a boat from the Woermann Line and headed for the arid coast of south-western Africa. They must have started the sea passage from a coastal town in northern Germany. Maybe they came together with other German soldiers.

I knew these details all too well, because this is how our family history had always been told by other members.[78] Interested in the German side of the family, Hedi had done some research on her own and remembered particulars of the German male members best. It was because of Hedi and Hans, that in 1976 during my first trip to Europe, I visited Irslingen and actually met a Dentlinger family there, who were quite surprised to hear about relatives of theirs existing in Namibia.

> The three friends entered the country and, so tradition has it in our family, a few years later my grandfather started a transport business.[79] With the aid of some camels, he would pick up supplies from ships docking at Swakopmund or Lüderitz Bucht and transport them over the Namib dunes along the well-known Bai-Weg, the generally accepted route for wagons through the Khomas Hochland Plateau, into the interior of the country. These trips would take him far and wide, apparently as far south as Bethanie. For it was in Bethanie that he met and married my grandmother, Sabina Olivier. Her father was said to have been Dutch and her mother Cape Malay. With that racial combination, she apparently was a striking beauty with long pitch-black silky hair, which she wore plaited down her back.

It may stretch the imagination of any reader to visualise our forefather, straight from Swabia in Württemberg, falling in love with this indigenous beauty only four years after his arrival in the country. What speaks for him, as Hedi told, is that

> he married her legally and officially in the mission church in Bethanie on 4 March 1896. I will always remember this day, because it is also my birthday.

This was an unusual step to take. As had been the case in the Cape, many German immigrants at the turn of the century were poor and only few could afford to "import" German girls to join them. Others did not have the inclination. In Namibia as in the rest of southern Africa, historical records abound with reports of men of European origin taking advantage of indigenous women and subsequently disappearing. Not so Gustav Dentlinger.

> They settled in Bethanie. He opened and successfully ran a hotel there.[80] I know of seven children being born from this prosperous union. One of them was my father, Hendrik, affectionately called Hennie by all. He was born in December 1896, nine months precisely after his parents were married.
>
> Even though my family in later years maintained connections to the south of the country particularly through marriages, my father came to settle in the Rehoboth, north of where he was born. So did his brothers. One remained in the hotel trade and opened a hotel at Rehoboth Station, a few kilometres outside Rehoboth.
>
> By the time I was born, our family owned large tracts of land south-west of Rehoboth. My father owned enough land to leave each of us five children an average-sized farm in the Rehoboth area when he died. He also owned another one in the south, near the present Namtses. But I am getting ahead of myself ...
>
> My mother was a strong-willed, proud woman of mixed genetic heritage. Anna Finster is what she called herself, ignoring her married name. She was fearless, difficult and many described her as arrogant. I found her strict, but very supportive of me and fair in her dealings. She bore my father seven children. Two of the boys died – one of blood poisoning during infancy and the second one during childhood. I was the only girl, born on 4 March 1932. The other four grew up making more or less successful lives for themselves. Possibly because I was still young and the only girl among the four remaining boys, I became my parents' favourite child.

All five of us grew up on Kwartel. I have very fond memories of that time. In contrast to what would happen later in my life, I felt safe, protected and loved.

It was not an impressive farm. Most farms in the area were relatively poor. My parents had built a single modestly sized room, as was the custom on farms, with a separate enclosure used as a kitchen, facing a dry riverbed. When I was still of preschool age, they could afford a grander house west of the dry riverbed. The old room remained on its original spot and was temporarily occupied by other family members. A windmill and the reservoir, our daily supply of water also stood on that spot. In the new house we had a little verandah from where we would watch the rain on those rare family occasions when it fell.

When it rained, too, we would immediately afterwards go down to the riverbed and see whether it was flowing. Sometimes, if the rain had been strong, we could watch big tree stumps being carried down by the current. But obviously this did not happen often.

I loved my father and we were very close. I would be the one whom he would take with him into the veld or to his beloved sheep. We would work together side by side, tending the animals, separating them or cutting hay for the dry season. When he taught me to drive our old Chevrolet, while I was still too small to reach the pedals, he would put me on his lap and show me how to switch gears, while he worked the pedals. Or we might go and camp in the veld at the *vlei*, recently filled by the rainwater, and spend a night in the open. This love of his would sustain me through the years, and it was his support, moral as well as financial, that in the hardest of moments helped me to overcome politically dangerous hurdles.

The children of farmers had to move to town to attend school, since then there were even fewer farm schools than there are now. So, when my brothers were of school-going age, we would spend our weeks in Rehoboth, and afterwards return to the farm for weekends and school holidays, much the way many families of the area still do today. At the appropriate time I also started school in Rehoboth. This proved to be the first incisive change in my life, having been free and uncomplicated up until then. In fact, I never did settle down in Rehoboth. With time the initial antipathy to my surroundings became full-grown dislike.

It was clear that I was different to the average Rehoboth student. Already then my family was considered more advantaged than other families in the area. On top of that, I stuck out like a sore thumb as a result of my looks. I was lighter in skin colour than most of my classmates. The texture of my hair was different, not so wavy. Even though some children had similar looks to mine, my facial features were finer than most. It was this combination that made people notice me.

Surprisingly, Rehobothers have remained intensely interested in each other's skin colour, linking it to family or genetic background.[81] They will take note of desirable or undesirable features and comment on them, using these physical features to assign people to categories, give them a status. One might have expected that because the Rehoboth community has been positioned low in a racially stratified society, it would therefore be sensitive to colour discrimination. Not so. Rehobothers have almost perfectly adopted the apartheid value system, whereby lighter is equated with better and darker with inferior.

Rehobothers also have a very pronounced class system, not unrelated to colour. As elsewhere, wealth is a criterion for being assigned to a higher class. Hedi was noticed for her European features, but also for coming from a relatively wealthy background. She was made to feel this confusing, but later painful, social separation early in life.

Even though I was sometimes being avoided, from what I can remember, my father was considered to be very much part of the community. He was well loved and generous, and people would constantly come to the farm to borrow money from him. In this way, he had acquired quite a status in the wider area. But he was also simply liked by many people. My mother considered herself somewhat above the average Rehobother, possibly because of the slightly elevated social standing, but perhaps also because of her part-German heritage. This was quite in accord with values at the time. She did not consider her stance to be in contradiction with her somewhat olive-coloured complexion.

There was this idea prevalent in the society, which then took root: if by luck you had fairly prominent Caucasian features, you stood a chance of escaping the present drab surroundings. Even more so, you could do better for yourself if you left Rehoboth and went to live in white society. This idea just seemed to float in the Rehoboth air. Soon I became aware of the fact that I could start a different life elsewhere. Once I had realised this, a kind of separation process started, whereby my mother would not let me play with other children of the neighbourhood. I was kept virtually locked up within the confines of the walled yard of our house. I learned early in life that my position would include being very lonely.

The odd teacher at school would encourage this process of making me feel separate from the community. "When the inspector comes, we will tell him that you are a child of poor whites, who cannot afford to send you to the white schools in Windhoek", I remember one of them saying once. After the hurtful laughter of the whole class had died down, I would look around me and ask myself: Do I really want to stay here for the rest of my life? Obviously I do not fit into the community I was born into.

Another more sympathetic teacher who understood my feeling of discomfort, said to me one day: "What a shame that a person like you should stay here". Other people, in accordance with these sentiments would say: "Pity that you should have to grow up in this environment". Or they would directly address my father: "Hennie, you should take your daughter away from here and expose her to other areas and people. She would have better chances there."

Influenced by the proud attitude of my mother and these people who were sympathetic to my disjointed existence, I allowed the idea of escaping my drab surroundings to grow in my mind. As time went on, I must admit it became quite an obsession. I would flee from here and settle in another part of the country, a white part. No other alternative existed for me any longer.

Already during the early fifties, people living in Rehoboth were farmers with a secondary residence away from the farm. At the best of times, Rehoboth was a hot, dry and dusty rural village with few diversions for young people. Obviously there were, and still are, people born and bred in Rehoboth who rightfully feel accepted and love it as their home. Unfortunately, because of her particular circumstances, Hedi was not one of them.

The only acceptable excitement in my childhood years were the occasional horseraces. The whole of Rehoboth would flock there on a weekend. The men would back their favourite horse, possibly win some money and for a few hours escape the usual dusty and drab monotony. I was attracted to the races for a different reason. At the age of about thirteen, I would prepare a twenty-five-litre metal can with cold water by wrapping wet cloths around it - the local cooler bag of the day. My father and I would load this together with a little table and bottles of orange juice concentrate called Oros, onto the car. At the racetrack I would set up my table at a convenient spot and sell my cool drinks, in my eyes making a small fortune.

For my father, the races were important because he owned some horses himself. Of course, it was special for him when one of his horses actually won.

Unfortunately, the races were only an annual diversion. At their conclusion, life continued on its drab course as set by the general social and cli-

matic conditions, but more so by the existing apartheid laws. These forbade any entertainment of any kind for us local Rehobothers in any so-
called white establishment anywhere. In fact even in Rehoboth, the races
were separated.

I remember vividly, for instance, how one day workers came to set up barricades to the entrance to the local post office. Until then this facility had
been used by all residents in a quite normal and peaceful manner. When
the workers were done, there was a separate entrance saying "whites
only" and yet another one stating "non-whites only". Many of us considered this a farce in a community which, to an overwhelming extent, was
made up of "non-whites". Shortly after the barricades had been set up,
they were torn down again by a few strong-minded residents, and
remained down for as long as I can remember.[82]

During the mid-1950s, the laws of racial separation were not yet tightly
enforced. An adventurous person could still escape from his or her present
surroundings and then take on a new identity in a different environment.
Hedi was playing with the idea of doing just that: moving into white society,
pretending to be a white person, in spite of being legally classified as coloured. This was referred to as "playing white". The final aim of this faking
process was to have your identification documents state that you were
white. This last step often became known as having "jumped the colour line".
The ironically light-hearted term in fact describes a very difficult and serious
process. There was nothing playful,[83] joyful or even simple about it. It was
less of a jump and more of a crawl. First of all, you needed the appropriate
physical appearance: a light skin colour, Caucasian facial features and ideally, straight, light-coloured hair. These were the very attributes Hedi had.
Then money was necessary – possibly to bribe officials, but also simply to
start a new life. This was particularly difficult, because in the 1940s it was
virtually impossible to obtain good schooling and job-training in Namibia
outside white areas.

But perhaps the saddest element of such a move was the emotional trauma of cutting yourself off from your own family. As hard as it is to imagine,
in most cases this was necessary. Your family would have the very characteristics, both physical and social, that you were trying to deny, such as curly,
dark hair, lack of linguistic fluency, lack of white education and social poise
appropriate to the white cultural environment. At best, you would not wish
to be seen in their company, because people who knew the signs of origin
would immediately draw conclusions. Difficult questions would have to be
answered. You would cringe, embarrassed for having been found out, but
secretly feel pained for having been forced to deny your own blood and the
people you loved.

The process of unlearning one set of behaviour and instantly exchanging it for another is extremely taxing. There was no trial period. This process is often referred to as "blending" in African-American literature, which aptly describes the need to fit in and not to stick out. Not to give yourself away. How great the humiliation if you used incorrect grammar or did not naturally know how to use a telephone. These were all tell-tale signs of your possible "true" heritage and you would feel mortified by not having paid sufficient attention to the details. It is thus understandable that many people who may have had a chance to transform themselves ethnically did not wish to do so. It requires tremendous psychological stamina, a good dose of courage, lack of fear of the many possible repercussions, and the ability to swallow potential humiliation and disappointments. In other words, only the most psychologically hardy could survive this trauma. Hedi already had experienced the loneliness of separateness that often also became part of this transformation.

At the time I was not thinking of the difficulties ahead. I was obsessed only with trying to make this escape into the "other" world.

My first chance came when I was sixteen years old. In those days, travelling salesmen (smouse) were a well-established part of farm life. They would visit particularly isolated farms and offer their goods either for money or barter to the rural families. They would sell fabric, shoes, clothes, conserved food. Farming legend has it that sometimes during years of severe drought, farmers would sell the bones of their dead animals to the smous in exchange for food. The smous who visited us sold a new invention at the time: a spray against mosquitos. He became my link to the outside world.

Coming from Johannesburg, this salesman would regularly stop at my father's farm. Over time he got to know all us children. On one such visit, he suggested to my father that he take me with him. I would be able to stay with him and his wife in the Transvaal. I was keen to do this. It seemed like the chance I had been waiting for, so naturally, I agreed to go with him. Preparations were made and I left the farm on 3 March 1949, amid tears.

The next day was my seventeenth birthday. As I saw it, my birthday present on this occasion was that for the first time in my life I slept in a hotel room. It was the one-horse town of Aroab in the south of Namibia, but to me it was the first step into my new life. The next evening my sympathetic hosts had another surprise in stall for me: the sight of the night lights of Johannesburg clearly visible from a surrounding hill. What a far cry these were from the petroleum lamps and flickering candles of the farm!

In retrospect, I am amazed at the chances I took, this being the first one. What security did I have as a young, inexperienced, shy girl of seventeen leaving home and putting myself at the mercy of virtual strangers? But as often in my life, I was extremely lucky. The salesman and his wife accepted me in a friendly and honest manner. They lived close to the mines in the Johannesburg area and soon I found a job in one of the shops as a saleslady. All went well. My hosts had in the meantime moved on, while I found work at the Koppie Alleen Mine and accommodation close by in the Bloemfontein area in the Orange Free State . After living alone for some eight months, I had to admit that I felt terribly homesick. I wrote home, saying that I wanted to return. My brother Hermann (your father) came to fetch me by train.

Now I was back on the farm, my longing for home was soon stilled, but where to go from here? Even though I had only completed my fifth grade, continuing my education in the Rehoboth school system was totally out of the question. Now I'd had a taste of the big, wide world - the big, wide, white world - and I was determined not to remain in Rehoboth. I became increasingly anxious because we were learning that apartheid laws were becoming more and more enforced. I felt that if I did not quickly make a decision, I would become stranded on the farm.

After kicking my heels for a while, I finally decided to go to Swakopmund. It seemed a good choice considering my purpose, because it was a haven for German Namibians. I soon found some work as a saleslady in a well-known grocery store. My employer was happy with my work and soon asked me to work in an affiliate store of his in Walvis Bay. There I sold men's clothing. This, of course, meant taking risks. Right from the start I now had to speak German. I had not learned it at school, nor at home, but had picked up a mere smattering here and there since it was widely spoken in Namibia. My proud mother had loved to brandish a few pet sayings like *"Arbeit macht das Leben süss"*, but obviously they didn't help much in my present predicament. I was far from being fluent, and was mortified when I used a phrase incorrectly or lacked the vocabulary to express myself. But in spite of these handicaps, I rented a room in the white part of town, used white public transport and worked in a white shop. All of this was illegal, and at any time I could have been told on. Even though this did ultimately happen, at least for the time being, I managed well.

In fact, thinking back to the years in Swakopmund, they were some of my happiest. The gentlemen coming into the store liked the way I served them. My employer was happy with my performance at work. From my rented room in Swakopmund, I would commute by trolley along the coast back and forth to work, a pleasant drive of a few miles between the two towns. In fact, I would increase my modest salary by buying some flowers in Swakopmund in the morning and selling them at a small profit to regular buyers in Walvis Bay. It paid the cost of my transport. This kind of commercial enterprise came to me naturally. It was just like helping my father selling his sheepskins or making money selling cool drinks at the horse-races.

With time, I met some young people with whom I would try out the different kinds of entertainment in Swakopmund. This was a natural urge, especially since there had not been entertainment of any kind back home. But I also realised that, had I come to Swakopmund as a coloured (my officially assigned ethnic group), all this enjoyment would have been denied me. I would not have been allowed to enter a Kaffee, the German-style coffee shop, to enjoy a cup of tea or coffee or eat at a white restaurant. I cherished the opportunity to walk the wide beautiful beaches. They provided ample opportunity for braais or barbeques. I enjoyed the German tradition of coffee and cake on Sundays. We went to cinemas to watch films, to hotels for drinks and chats and dances. It seemed like heaven!

I was pretending to be white, but also playing with my luck. Naturally, this was not to last forever. One day my landlady came to me and wanted to talk to me. "Fräulein Hedi," she said seriously. I immediately knew this meant trouble. "I received a letter here ... an anonymous letter, which tells me that you originate from Rehoboth. Is this true?"

The implications of the unasked questions scared me. She was pointing out that I had actually contravened the law. Of course, I wondered about the anonymity of the letter.

"Yes, it is so. I am from Rehoboth," I told her, but I also told her why I was here; that I wanted a better life for myself, to explore opportunities denied me in Rehoboth, that I wanted to earn a decent income. Was there anything wrong with that? Were these not normal dreams of young people anywhere, at any time? If, however, she wanted me to leave, I would do so. "No", she answered. "You have always been a good tenant. I have been happy with you living in my house and, as far as I am concerned, you should stay as long as you like." Again I had been lucky. I had good and courageous people on my side. I continued living on her premises for a long time.

However, not everyone was so tolerant and understanding. For instance, I remember vividly a day when, in a coffee shop just outside Swakopmund, an elderly gentleman walked in. He greeted me in a friendly manner, because I knew him from visits to our farm. A few days later I received a phone call from my father in Rehoboth. Always concerned to be on the right side of the law, he admonished me for having been seen in a white establishment. I asked him what he wanted me to do. I had to come to Swakopmund to improve my opportunities in life. In my eyes, this included going out with others, and these others happened to be white. I could not believe that this man had told on me, after he had plentifully enjoyed our hospitality on the farm.

Now years afterwards and with the wisdom of age at my side, I cannot help wondering about the process of moving from one group to another like this. In effect, in those times in Namibia, it meant moving from one racial environment to another. In Rehoboth I had felt ostracised, as if a certain section of the community wished me to leave because my looks were unacceptable. But on the other side of the racial divide, so to speak, I was not allowed either. Where was I to belong then? Into which group was I to be included?

However, it gives me tremendous satisfaction to reminisce about those individuals who were supportive and who readily offered their help. For instance, I remember a magistrate in Johannesburg at a social event once warning me about the increasing tightening of racial classifications. He offered to assist me "getting my papers in order", a euphemism for chang-ing the racial classification on my identity documents. This would have been illegal, no doubt punishable in one form or another. I never did take up his offer, yet he offered his help despite the dangers involved for him.

Before these two events, my time in Swakopmund had held many surpris-es and prospects. I belonged to a pleasant circle of friends, including some very eligible young men. But I was hesitant. I needed a man I could depend on. Then one man in particular showed his interest in me. We started see-ing more of each other. I felt I needed to tell him about my background – where I came from – before it got too serious. At the same time, a good friend of the family came to Swakopmund specifically to let me know that the apartheid laws were becoming increasingly tight. My friend told me that if I was serious about this young man, I should marry him before it becomes impossible. I responded: "Well, I have my pride too. I am not going to ask a man to marry me." But I did invite him to come home with me to meet my family before we got further involved.

Hedi's situation is perhaps hard for others to understand today. But it per-fectly reflects the sentiments of that time for people like us. As a girl from a mixed background, I also had to inform the boys of my choice about my her-itage. Nobody told us to do so; it was simply expected. It made us feel embar-rassed, inadequate, socially misplaced, inferior ... all at once. We felt guilty. "For what?" I ask myself now, but then it was all different. The tacit argument was that coming from a mixed background was something defiling, and that the boys had all the right to know before the relationship became too serious. It was also tacitly understood that the man might decide to call off the friendship because he was scared of legal repercussions or social stigma. It did not occur to us for a moment that other features or characteristics in the choice of a partner may play an equal, if not a more important role. What about factors such as intelligence, personality or education? What about love? We were so fixated on our ethnic background that alternatives totally eluded us.

But the day actually turned out fine. I remember that at one point, we went for a walk up the little hill opposite the house. Hans told me that he loved me and as long as he could be with me, he did not care about my family background.

I was happy. We both moved to Walvis Bay and each rented a room. He worked for a well-known businessman in town, a Mr Laing. I continued working for Baumgarten. Soon Hans was able to buy himself a Henschel lorry.

Nature took its course and it did not take long for us to become really close. Hans had his work and I had mine, but both paid only a modest salary. To improve this situation, Hans would collect crushed stones for construction from a quarry during the weekend, drive it to the commercial section of Walvis Bay and sell a load at a time. Soon he started doing this independently. We did not earn much this way, but every extra pound helped, and working together strengthened our relationship. Late on a Sunday we would wash and buff our truck, to have it ready for action during the coming week, when he needed it for his regular employment. It was a pleasant routine. The only dampening factor was that we had to be careful not to appear together too often in public. Always, at the back of our minds, was the fear of being found out or being told on. So far we had been lucky.

We continued this work routine until January 1954, at which time - to my horror - I discovered I was pregnant. This increased our problems horrendously. We had a relationship "across the colour bar" as the saying went, a serious contravention of the Immorality Act of 1927, as revised in 1950, punishable with imprisonment. And I was now carrying live, tangible proof of such a relationship. Furthermore, the child would have to remain illegitimate since we could not marry, a solution normally chosen by myriads of young couples all over the world who found themselves in this situation. Not so in Namibia then: we belonged to different racial groups and were forbidden to marry according to the Mixed Marriages Act of 1949. Once our child was born we would have to face the issue of having to register the child according to some legal racial classification.

After endless discussions, we decided we would escape to Angola …

We agreed to take whatever chances needed to be taken: we would have our child there and register the birth in Angola, which meant there would be no need to specify any racial category at all. We planned to open a garage and drive building material as we had done in Walvis Bay. Otherwise we would see what other possibilities existed for us there.

We were young then, and on top of it all, we were poor. Our efforts during the weekends did not earn us huge sums, nor did our individual jobs. As would often be the case, I would have to depend on my family to help me in this time of need. I got in touch with my parents and arranged that I would come to the farm before we left.

When we arrived on Kwartel, my proud mother stood at the front gate of the yard at the end of the garden to welcome us. In spite of my good rela-tionship with my father, he and my brothers had driven into the veld. They obviously felt unable to face this embarrassing situation. I also remember clearly that on this occasion, my mother gave me three hundred pounds. That was a lot of money in those days and it proved her support for me, even under those dubious circumstances. This was the last item in our preparations before leaving Namibia. I had said goodbye to my mother; we had sold our faithful Henshel and bought a five-ton International instead. Now we were ready. All this had taken us a while and I was now eight months along in my pregnancy.

The drive to San da Bandeira, the present-day Lubango, was a harrowing experience! With the International packed with our few belongings, we braved the corrugated gravel roads for four days. I remember Hans stretching his free hand over to me, holding me down in my seat every time we hit another deep pothole to stop me from being hurled into the air. My legs were badly swollen, and by the time we finally arrived, I did not feel at all well. The date for the birth was set for within a week. The doctor in San da Bandeira suggested I rest and get the swelling in my legs down. Hans insisted I stay in the hotel for that week. Once I was better, we drove on to Lubido where we knew another German couple, the Schmidts. We did not have long to wait for the birth of the baby. Thank goodness Hans had found a hospital that was prepared to take me. On a Sunday we checked in, somewhat early but nervous about my condition after the long trip.

On Monday 13 September 1954 our first son was born. The hospital personnel insisted I stay in bed at least until the following Friday. While I was busy with the baby, Hans explored possibilities of staying in Angola.

The Schmidts were keen for us to remain, and had even staked out a plot on the banks of the Kunene River. We were seriously contemplating the possibility of realising our plans: transporting gravel here with our faithful pick-up truck as we had done in Walvis Bay. Hans had gone to talk to the authorities in this regard – but it was not to be. The immigration official wanted to know why Hans was German and held a South African passport.[84] We would be able to stay if we could prove we had a hundred thousand pounds to start up a business in Angola. Otherwise they were giving us a month or two (I've forgotten the details) to leave the country. They considered this lenient in the light of us having a newborn baby. Our German friends trusted us to such an extent that they offered us the use of their own hundred thousand pounds, "Just to show them that you have the money," they insisted. We greatly appreciated their trust and generosity. Hans went with Mr Schmidt to the authorities to register, but the same question was brought up: why was he German, but holding a South African passport?

Once the five compulsory days for staying in the hospital were over, we headed back southwards on the same bumpy roads to an uncertain future in the country we had left.

By now it was October 1954. Once back in Namibia, we did not return to Swakopmund, but settled in Karibib instead, a small town almost halfway on the route between Windhoek and Swakopmund. Hans started a job in the local marble quarry now transporting marble blocks with his International. Of course we had very little money and no accommodation, so we decided to rent a little room in the only hotel in Karibib. We put the baby in a wooden apple box, lined it with a soft base of baby blankets and a small pillow. He fitted in perfectly and was none the worse for it. In that one room we slept, cooked and ate, and it served as a living room during the day. While Hans worked, I tended to myself and the baby. It was not altogether unpleasant.

Unfortunately we were not left to pursue this peaceful existence. The police had got wind of us, and in their effort to enforce apartheid laws, were on our trail. Later we were to find out this had been going on for a while. They had lost us when we had left for Angola, but then had once again caught up with us in Karibib. All of this we gathered from warnings that were passed on to us by some trustworthy people. I can no longer remember how much we knew ourselves about the police observing us.

But before it got serious, we were to have a little fun, which, even in later years, Hans and I would continue to have.

As was often the case, we had made friends with another family who were renting the room next to ours. The Schneiders had fled from East Germany and were trying to start a new life in Namibia. In December during the hot summer, a time when the heat is so unbearable in the interior of the country that all and sundry flock to the coast, Hans suggested we take our pick-up truck and spend a few days camping at Henties Bay, in those years a small place north of Swakopmund. We thought we would be relatively safe from any police persecution there on the deserted open beaches. The Schneiders had two girls, one seven and one four years old. The seven of us soon set off happily anticipating our first holiday together. Once there we pitched our modest camp: one family slept inside the truck, the other underneath it. The cool, breezy sun-drenched days were spent with the men trying their luck at catching fish for our evening pot, while we, the two mothers, occupied ourselves with the children.

When we returned to Karibib after our vacation, my father phoned a friend, asking him to walk over to the hotel and bring us the following message: "The police are after you. They have been ordered to arrest you." A sergeant, who was a friend of my father's had told him: "Hennie, they are looking for your daughter. I wanted to warn you; you better make sure that she leaves Karibib." A truly brave and loyal man! This is all he could say, because it was, of course, not exactly in his line of duty.

Some days later my brother, Hermann, your father, arrived. Then one balmy evening – Hans having gone on some apparent errand – I quietly passed the baby through the window to Hermann standing on the outside, and I casually walked out of the front door of the hotel. Our plan was for the police watching this to assume I was without the child and wouldn't be going far. Instead, I jumped into the car waiting around the corner and we drove off to the farm. Some time later, Hans came sauntering in after his apparent errand, and to all appearances prepared himself for a peaceful night's sleep. I was thankful that whatever may happen, our baby would be safe on the farm with my mother.

The next day Hans continued with his daily routine of going to work. In the afternoon he had to go to the post office. As he came out, he was suddenly surrounded by police. "We are here to arrest you."

"But wait – not so fast. I want to see my lawyer first!" This was allowed, after which he was taken to the local police station and asked to pay fifty pounds bail. By that time the baby and Hermann and I were already on Kwartel.

Of course, the saga continued. One day the sympathetic sergeant drove up to our farmhouse on Kwartel and said to my father: "Hennie, I did warn you and I am sorry to have to do this, but I have come to arrest your daughter!"

"Yes, you did warn me. She is ready. I have only one favour to ask you. Could I drive her to the police station myself?" My father could not stand the humility of seeing me being taken there in the back of the police van. The gentle policeman agreed to our request, even though he added that this was totally contrary to the law. He was allowing it because of the respect my father had in his eyes and in the eyes of the community.

And even though generally I am a terrible coward, at that moment - before God! - I was not scared one little bit. I took off my rings and said, "Here I am. I am ready."

We drove to Rehoboth, my father and I ahead, the sergeant behind us. Once there the appropriate documents were filled in and after some deliberation, I was allowed to go home on bail.

Many years later we would laugh about the fact that at the time of his arrest, Hans did not have the required fifty pounds on him to pay his bail. He had not been to the bank, which of course did not concern the police much. But they did allow him to contact a friend to borrow the money. It was after this that he must have contacted van der Maade to elicit his services for our case.

The time before the actual court case is a total blur for me. All I remember is sitting on the farm, worrying about Hans, tending to our son and waiting for the date of the trial to be announced. I did not see Hans until that memorable night before the court case in Karibib, when we sneaked away for a few minutes on our own.

The so-called "trial" the next day was almost an anticlimax. After all these many months of worry and fear of being caught by the police, in the end I felt empty and tired. The magistrate came in and opened the court proceedings. I clearly remember van der Maade getting up and asking the magistrate: "Sir, looking at this woman, would you consider her to be a coloured person or a white person?"

The magistrate answered: "I would consider her a white person."

We could hardly believe that, with these words spoken, we had won our case! Van der Maade had built his argument on obtaining this simple opinion from the magistrate. Whereas we had entered the court as criminals, now we were free to go, free to get married, free to live where we chose and free to send our child to whatever school we wanted. There were still some administrative details that had to be completed by van der Maade.

For one, my identity documents had to be changed to finally indicate that I was now by law classified as white.

Another thing van der Maade did for us was to arrange our wedding. Why he did this, I do not remember. Perhaps he was simply a good person and felt he wanted to see this issue closed. The day before the wedding, my brother Hermann and I had set out from the farm once again. We met Hans in Karibib, where he had remained. The three of us left for Swakopmund and a simple wedding in a small Evangelical church in town. We were married there on 15 June 1955. Hermann acted as witness. There were no celebrations. I did not even have a bouquet of flowers. For this, the most important day of my life, I wore a light coloured suit to the ceremony. But we did not mind at all that it was a simple wedding. For us, the happiness lay in knowing that we were to be married legally and could now live a recognised life as husband and wife. We spent our wedding night in a hotel in Swakopmund.

After the wedding, we briefly returned to Karibib. My father had given us, as was the custom, a little farm in the area together with three hundred sheep and the loan of seventy head of cattle. The idea of this was to help us get onto our feet to start farming and earn some money, for instance by creaming the milk from the cows and selling it.

We decided on running the farm rather and made a reasonable success of it. Late in that year, I found out that I was pregnant again. We felt somewhat uncomfortable. Although the court case had made it possible for us to become legally married, we didn't feel quite at home in the Rehoboth community, nor did I feel totally accepted by Hans's family. With the new pregnancy, all of these thoughts came to a head. Even though we were grateful to my father for giving us a source of income, we asked ourselves whether it had been wise to have come here in the first place. Should we not leave and try our luck elsewhere? Perhaps there was an equally good income to be made outside Namibia. Possibly different surroundings would be more beneficial for our second child. As was the case with our son, to be born away from the present environment simply gave the child a better chance; no questions of background would even arise.

We had on a previous occasion been to Zimbabwe (then Rhodesia) and Nyasaland for a brief holiday. Now we were wondering whether we should not go there again. Without much ado, we made arrangements to leave. We did not sell the farm, though. It remained under my father's control. I got my papers in order and we left for Rhodesia. Our daughter was born there on 28 November 1956. I came home briefly for the funeral of my father in 1957. When we then went back, you came with us – do you remember?

She looked at me, her forehead in wrinkles. I nodded. "And after that you came to settle in Windhoek," I reminded her.

> Yes, you know that we stayed in Rhodesia for four years, before we finally came back to settle in Windhoek in 1960. Our second son was born here on 20 April 1962. I have now lived in this house since 1976 … over thirty years! They were happy years, mostly because of the success we made of our life together, Hans and I. We had a happy marriage, until Hans died in 1992.

In March 2016, Hedi and I sat and talked for the last time, the week before her eighty-fourth birthday. She finished her story by saying:

> I am happy that our three children grew up to lead normal lives and that their children could grow up to live happy lives. I am proud of what I have achieved. I am now eighty-three. And this is what I get my joy from, our happy family life … over the years.

I remembered our first extended talk back in 1997. We had sat talking on her cool verandah for some days then. It felt good now. I felt closer to her than I had for a long time. Our relationship had not always been easy. Our views about our heritage were different, particularly in retrospect.

At the time of our long talk, Namibia had been independent for six years and apartheid dismantled for the same length of time. She had returned to Rehoboth from Rhodesia for the funeral of her father, and once more from Windhoek for her mother's funeral. Other than that, she had rarely if ever been back.

I needed to know from Hedi whether, in her mind, this severe sacrifice had been worth it. She confidently answered:

> Yes it was. I could shape my life the way I wanted to, and not the way the government with its laws had prescribed.

I could not help but feel a tremendous sadness for her. Our paths had been similar. Was it because, being almost twenty years her junior, I was able to reinvent myself? Or because I had been less in the crossfire than she was? I grew up already beyond the colour line; thankfully I was spared the kind of decisions she had to make. I did not have to give up my immediate family and bear the heartache of the loss. To all intents and purposes, I was white. I had to deal with the situation retrospectively, as it were. My heart went out to her for the pain of having had to deny such a large and seminal part of her life.

I ask myself how many individuals and families have had to do this in our land and I grieve for their suffering and pain. I see how unnatural and fundamentally unhealthy it has been – psychologically – for all those who have gone through this process. And, as my cousin pointed out and we all know, many South Africans have gone through worse. I look at my wider family and discover how those who remained, faced the ethnic music and moved with it, were able to shape a happier medium for themselves, at least in Namibia.

5   MY STORY

Hedi's drama must have caused quite a stir in the rather isolated, mundane existence at Kwartel, where the only amusement was of the family's own making, such as when ou Lenas would teach me Khoe sentences inappropriate for my age. Visitors came rarely. Strangers had no reason to brave the rough farm roads joining the sprawling Dentlinger farms. When on a rare occasion the whining of a car engine was heard, all would take note long before the vehicle had manoeuvred the last dip to the Prosopis trees and finally come to stop at Anna Finster's yard. As a rule it would turn out to be either the *smous,* or family. This is how it must have been before Hedi's adventures. Perhaps this was one of the reasons she left. But, in spite of its dreariness, it was home for both of us, albeit at different times.

One rare occasion of family socialising happened at the end of December 1951. My aunt, Elisabeth Benade, had come to celebrate the end of the year, but also wanted to be there for the birth of her older sister's first child (me). As was the tradition, one of the elderly Khoe-speaking women, possibly ou Lenas, had recently massaged my highly pregnant mother and must have noticed that a birth was imminent. She had warned my father. But I'm told there was a rare atmosphere of joviality at the time; somebody was even playing the *konsertina* - harmonica. So, even when the birth pains came on strong and at regular intervals, it took quite some persuasion to have my father leave the festivities to drive my mother to the Catholic hospital in Rehoboth forty kilometres away. Perhaps the corrugations and stones in the road helped, for I did everyone a favour and arrived without complications on 31 December. This allowed for the celebrations to be continued a few days later.

At the time when Hedi and Hans were agonising over their future, I was three-and-a-half years old. We lived in the little red brick house on the other side of the gully that, as a child, Hedi would cross after the rain together with her father. It was said by some relative that my grandfather had built it for my parents when my mother fell pregnant. It was the house to which ou Lenas and ou Marias would come to drink their tea, socialising while my mother worked. I was much too young to have grasped any of the dramatic events playing themselves out on the farm, or their final happy resolution for Hedi and her Hans. Yet I have vague memories of odd nightly comings and goings, which I sensed at the time to be connected with the two of them. Nobody talked about any of this in my presence. There would have been a lot of hushed conversation among the women as they bent over their chores. Repeated tut-tuts and shaking of heads, worried glances and heavy sighs, would have been tell-tale signs that everything was not in order on the family front. I may have asked for a small favour, maybe for a suddenly needed

*My parents
on their
wedding day,
25 January 1944*

glass of water. I would have been told unusually harshly: "Why don't you taaake yourself a cup of water and then go and play outside. We are now busy!"

"Why don't you go and play outside." This statement was never posed as a question. It was not even a rhetorical question. It was, in fact, a command: Go and play outside! We don't want to be disturbed! We are now involved in our own conversation, which is "not meant for the ears of children", this being another phrase often directed at me by the women. Of course their talk revolved around topics sexual and matters of procreation. This I could tell by the smiles and smirks and instant quiet should I appear, or else by a quick change of subject which they thought I didn't notice. I understood then that I was dispatched outside so that they could thoroughly immerse themselves in an extended *skinnering* - gossiping session.

And why did I not want to "go and play outside"? Because *vlakte* - barren desert - is what there was outside. There were no playmates and scarcely any toys to play with. In all my life as a child, I remember having two dolls. From much later I remember a tea set which I was very fond of, and would get my mother and anyone else there to pretend to drink tea from. Those were the only toys I ever possessed. Mostly I was left to my own devices. I remember playing on a stone ridge just at the end of the yard. I would line up glass shards I had found lying around, sorting them according to colour, shapes and sizes. There was no garden. There might have been a struggling oleander bush in front of our house, but nothing like the garden of Anna Finster.

Hedi must have experienced similar treatment as a child growing up on Kwartel. In fact, we had other things in common. Both of us were born in Rehoboth, both of us virtually grew up and lived in the area until school-going age. The grand-parental house on Kwartel had been Hedi's home until she finally left in 1955. The blonde, blue-eyed, tall brother she mentioned as having accompanied her during the trial in Karibib and again at her wedding was my father. She was, of course, much older than I and had left Kwartel by 1955. In fact, I only really got to know her when I lived with her and her young family in Zimbabwe.

I would, however, still spend many happy months before this came about. Etched in my memory are the occasions of listening to records with Anna Finster. I can no longer pinpoint the exact year, but I remember walking down to her house through the little gully and up the other side, entering her garden along the straight stone path and maybe finding her sitting on the cool, dark verandah or pottering in the kitchen. If the mood was right, she would find her old gramophone, His Master's Voice, in one of the bedrooms. She would set it on a table, ready for using. I can still smell the black plastic it was made of, see the shining sharpness of the needle at the end of the wound arm. Then she would go and get two seven-single records she had. She would place one on the turntable, lift the arm with its silver head backwards and thereby make the record start turning. A few seconds would pass and – miracle upon miracle – the penetrating voice of Melina Mercouri would proclaim *"Ich bin ein Mädchen aus Piräus und liebe den Hafen, die Schiffe und das Meer ..."* Then the deep baritone of Freddie Quinn lamented "Jimmy Brown *das war ein Seemann und das Herz war ihm so schwer ..."* The incongruity of German pop songs with marine themes, blaring out into the air of the dry, hot, semi-desert of the Basterland must have been momentous. That my grandmother, who did not speak more than a handful of German words, would be playing German records was not as surprising as the fact that she had found these exotic musical items in the first place. The gramophone today belongs to my cousin. The origin of the records, long since lost, nobody was able to tell. Perhaps she ordered them from the *smous* with whom Hedi went to Johannesburg. At any rate, they must have been the most often played tracks of Melina Mercouri and Freddy Quinn ever.

For many years we remained a poor family. It was only in the late fifties – when my father found work on the Cordon, the veterinary fence constructed to contain domestic stock from spreading foot-and-mouth disease – that we came to some form of financial means. Even after that, I would have placed us in the lower economic class, at most lower middle. Being stock farmers during the early 1950s and owning no land, we had to be mobile, much as pastoralists had been during the previous century. My elderly aunts will often finish relating a story with the phrase "and this is how we moved around". One trekked in search for jobs, opportunities or pasture for stock. In this way we came to rent pasture on two different farms in the south of Namibia. One was called *Namtses*, the other *Verlos* (release). This was a bad joke of a name, for there was never a release of any kind on any farm.

Namtses and Verlos were close to Gamis where my mother and her siblings had grown up. From one of these farms I remember the sugarcane reeds that grew around the reservoir. The grown-ups would cut off stalks and give pieces of these to me to chew on. By biting onto them and pulling them through my clenched teeth, I would squeeze out the sweet pulp. I loved doing this. Raw sugar rated close to sweets, and sweets were only ever seen at Christmas, and then only in the form of brightly coloured liquorice squares and roles.

During the poor years, family members would support each other financially or by pooling their resources. Since the rented farms were close to my mother's home, it is likely that land was jointly rented and the herd jointly owned with male relatives of hers.[85] This might be the reason why they came from nearby Gamis for the shearing. Her brother Albert Enssle came, as did John, a stepbrother. When the time came one day, instead of driving the flock into the veld, the animals would be enclosed in a *kraal* – a pen – alongside the old reservoir on the riverbank. There, the men would each catch a sheep by one of its hind legs, and lodge it between their own legs in a kind of sitting position. Holding the animal with his knees, draping the front legs over his left arm, each man would commence to rhythmically cut layers of wool starting from the belly of the sheep and working his way around to the back. As the wool tumbled off the shears in layers, it would be picked up and thrown into huge hessian holding bags, so big that they were suspended from poles extending a few metres off the ground. One of the men would lift me up high and drop me into the wool in the hessian bags. It was my job to compact the wool by treading down on it. I remember the oiliness, the strong smell of the dirt and dust in it, and the feeling of the thorns and bits of twigs that had remained stuck in the sheep's coats as they pricked and scratched my legs and feet. I would jump up high above the top of the containing hessian wall, and let myself fall down into the soft fleece, much like one would jump on a trampoline. It was a liberating feeling, the wind lifting my hair on the downward fall. This was another rare occasion of enjoyment and socialising in an otherwise quite boring and uneventful daily routine.

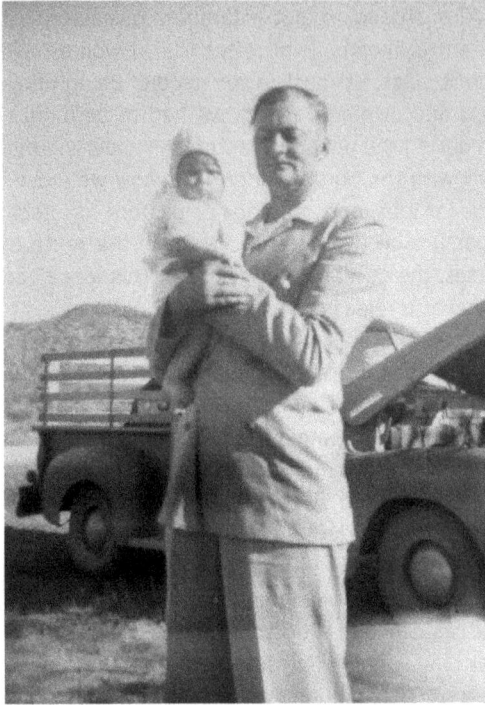

My father with myself, May 1952

A less pleasant memory I have of the farm Namtses, is how I got my first hiding from my father. It has always been a tradition in rural Namibia [86] and even in southern Africa that the employer's children would play with employee's children. This seemed logical. Farms being as isolated as they were, there were no other children around in a radius of many miles. My mother certainly had done so, and so would I. We would shape miniature oxen from the river clay and line them up in the sand. Another game we played was to kneel in the sand and alternatively shift our knees and shins forward, making what we considered to be car tracks in the sand. We could spend hours filling a large area in the sand with such tracks.

Out of the blue, when one day I came home from such a pleasant bout of playing, my father told me that I was not to play with black children and proceeded to spank me. Since I was only ever spanked twice in my life as a child, both times by my father, it seems significant that I should remember this incident fifty-six years later. It is difficult to say today what I felt then. I cannot even remember whether it was a particularly hard spanking. It must have been the emotional impact that left an indelible mark on me. All in all, I must have been very surprised, but even more confused. On the whole my younger sister and I had been brought up in a decidedly anti-authoritarian manner, a very modern approach for the mid-1950s. We didn't really know corporal punishment at all. I would have been pained by the unfairness of such a severe and unusual reprimand. I probably had considered our games a rather inventive way of filling my time of "go and play outside".

Above all, however, this must have been the very first time that I came face to face with this type of ethnic prejudice. At the age of about four I probably was still totally colour blind. I might have put a clean dishcloth on ou Lenas's lap before sitting on it, but I'm sure I did not understand the implication of this behaviour. Mostly I would have seen us all as being very similar, intertwined in our daily lives. The adults worked together, conversed with each other, helped each other. As I've already mentioned, my parents and most adults around me spoke Khoe naturally. I must have silently questioned how our playing together was any different from ou Lenas and ou Marias visiting at our house or treating us during an illness. True to family habit, no discussion followed this incident – at least I do not remember any.

In later years I would continue to notice this ethnic prejudice in my father, a prejudice that was inexplicable and foreign to me. It is now too late to ask him what moved him to hold some in such low regard, for instance, the Khoe-speaking employees, and yet others in higher esteem, Caucasian-looking blondes. I do remember, though, that virtually until the day he died in November 2011, true to Rehoboth tradition, he believed that European physical features were desirable, giving the bearer a higher status in his estimation.[87] He might say "you need not be ashamed of her", implying that the woman he spoke of looked white and not Khoe or negroid; or he would beat our Khoe-speaking shepherd severely with a *sjambok,* a short leather whip, if any sheep had gone missing.[88] I do not remember any real discussion between my father and the herder of possible reasons for the missing sheep. He seemed, in my memory, to have at the outset made up his mind that the herder "had fallen asleep" while he should have been watching the sheep. One could now ask oneself whether this punishment was an expression of an employer-employee relationship or was it motivated by ethnicity? Would my father have whipped a white or a fellow Rehoboth sheepherder so readily or severely? Would he perhaps have considered the neglect differently, if he himself had possessed less European features?

I never asked questions relating to prejudice while doing my family research. It just never came up. One would hope that the kind of discrimination of the past no longer exists. Pearson writes about this phenomenon during the seventies: "The way in which colour, class, prejudice and discrimination interact in Rehoboth is quite complex, and an understanding of the interaction [of these] is essential in order to explain this apparent paradox".[89] From my experience of the Gebiet during the fifties and sixties, I can add to Pearson's comment that I remember Khoe-speaking male employees

My mother at Kwartel Wes, early 1960s

mostly having been treated very curtly, almost dismissively by my male relatives. They were often ridiculed or teased. By contrast, the relationship between female employers and their female domestic helpers seemed more collegial. The women would stand by each other during illness, more so during the illness of children. They would seek out each other's company, as ou Lenas did on her visits to my mother. Would it have been more difficult for Rehoboth men than women to have a normal relationship with Khoe-speaking people? Did Rehoboth men feel they had to set themselves apart from their Khoe-speaking employees more clearly than women did? In my child's-eye view, my mother would work together with any domestic help quite naturally. She seemed totally non-judgemental. So, whereas my mother never so much as lifted a finger towards us, the hiding from my father had many layers of meaning.

After Namtses, we returned to Kwartel to continue living in that little red brick house looking down upon Anna Finster's bigger house and garden. In 1957 my grandfather, Hennie, died at the age of sixty-one. He had been a popular man because of his gentle nature and generosity. Considered wealthy, he was able to leave each of his children land and some money. This was in contrast to the normal practice in the Gebiet where farms were subdivided, in order for each child to inherit a portion.[90] Hans, my favourite uncle, was given Tierkolkies south of Kwartel. Auchab, a farm just under two thousand hectares west of Rehoboth, and another parcel of land elsewhere and some money was bequeathed to Hedi. Stephanus was given Khunub. His youngest son Adolph was to inherit Kwartel once my grandmother had

My sister at Kwartel Wes, early 1960s

passed away. For the time being, she remained living on it. My father was given Kwartel Wes, a farm of nearly six thousand hectares to the west of Kwartel and Rehoboth, which had been bought from a German couple, the Welsteins. From then onwards, an enclave of Dentlingers was to be found stretching south-west of Rehoboth.

Inheriting Kwartel Wes was a big step towards a degree of financial independence – but it did not lift us out of poverty. Even though we were now landowners, this did not reflect in the architecture of our humble home. In fact, there were some elements that were downright unusual.

We took over the lineal domicile on Kwartel Wes as the Welsteins had built and occupied it. Two equally sized adjoining rooms and a third slightly longer at a right angle to these formed an L shape. A flat, corrugated iron roof extended beyond the walls and covered a narrow verandah. From each room a door opened onto said verandah, closing the L shape into a rectangle. The living room at the short end of the L was the "usual heavy-handed ... attempt at respectability"[91], as Athol Fugard tells of his own childhood home. Entrance to it was reserved for Sunday lunch, visitors and Christmas celebrations. It was furnished with a low sideboard of dark wood, which – I was happy to see – still exists on Kwartel Wes today. The open shelf of the sideboard held delicate wineglasses with globular bases, of which I possess the last two, but also glasses each decorated with a ring of strawberries around their tops. I cannot remember us ever having used these cherished items, probably one of few things my mother had brought into the marriage. Two framed prints hung on the wall opposite the door. One of these, I believe, was a rather dark depiction of Berchtesgaden, the origin of which, no doubt, also was the household of my German maternal grandfather, Albert Enssle. Certainly in the mid-fifties in the Gebiet, I am convinced nobody in my family knew that it depicted Hitler's favourite holiday recluse. A dining-room table with six chairs stood on a linoleum floor of grey and white checkerboard squares. As a rule, the mustard-coloured curtains remained tightly drawn across the single window.

The adjoining room was the kitchen. This is where we lived. It had a mud and dung floor, which was sprinkled with water and then swept each day to fight the dust. This type of flooring was directly taken over from Khoe speakers, who would line the floors of their huts in this manner.[92] Mud and dung floors, however, were not unusual in the rural areas of both Namibia and South Africa. As had been the case on Kwartel, on Kwartel Wes, too, a wood stove was used for cooking, or else the small primus stove that needed to be pumped. A kitchen table stood against a wall and odd shelves hid an assortment of jars, cans and enamel eating utensils behind hand-sewn curtains faded by frequent washing and drying under the merciless Namibian sun. The zinc pails holding drinking water stood on similar wooden crates next to the door. In fact, most of the shelf-like, cupboard-like furniture was constructed of wooden boxes originally having held cans of paraffin oil. These boxes would be joined vertically or horizontally and covered with some white cloths sown from flour bags.

As on Kwartel, here too, my mother and I would walk early in the morning before the intense heat of midday, to the wind pump and reservoir some five hundred metres from the house. Just like any Khoe-speaking woman, we would carry these pails on our heads, supported by a fabric ring. I am happy to say we were quite good at this, usually not spilling a single drop, even when lowering the full pails onto the ground.

A functional second stable door opened to the backyard with its woodpile, washing line and outside hearth protected by a clump of agaves. We would eat outside as often as we would in the kitchen. It was the family tradition to *braai* – barbeque – when a sheep or a goat had been slaughtered. From the fresh carcass and in the absence of any reliable cooling facilities, the first meal would be the relatively lean liver, halved and seasoned with only salt and pepper. To compensate for its leanness, the small intestine, turned inside out and meticulously cleaned was laced with a strip of fat, again spiced just with salt and pepper. This complemented the liver. After the flames of the fire had died down and the coals were glowing deep orange, first the intestine and only later the liver were laid on the *rooster* – the grill. We would sit at the fire on our haunches or on little wooden benches, staring at the fire with anticipation of these delicacies. The smoke curled above our heads, the meat crackled over the coals, while our salivary glands worked. When finally it was ready, we children would intermittently be given pieces of crispy fatty intestine together with the liver, as the grownups cut and ate with a sharp pocketknife.

Within the circle of light from the fire, the dogs were lying and anxiously waiting. Now and then they would be thrown a less valued piece of meat or, if other pieces were grilled, a bone, which they instantaneously leapt for from their lying positions, following its flight in an arc through the air. Their crunching of the bones and growling in defence of a chunk of meat would underline the chirping of the cicadas and the occasional moaning of the cattle in the kraal in the dark beyond the light of the fire.

After my sister was born, the third room adjoining the kitchen and entered from the verandah was reserved as bedroom for me. It had a bed in it, a big table and the usual paraffin box shelves. My "bed-time stories" on Kwartel Wes in that little room consisted of my mother sitting next to me on the bed and us chatting about any kind of topic that came to mind, until I finally fell asleep. She would then return to the kitchen next door and continue her chores usually until late at night. If I woke up again, I would always hear her handling the pots and pans and see her shadow move on the verandah floor as it reflected in the light of the paraffin lamp.

Before moving to that little room, I would sleep in the same beds as my parents in the *rondavel*, a round room with metal walls. *Rondavels* are often used as employee accommodation on farms, no doubt because they are cheap. The concept of a *rondavel* has become a popular element in southern African architecture and can be found constructed of the most sophisticated materials. Not ours. The circular room with pointed roof of soldered sheet metal was unbearably hot in summer and freezing cold in winter. I have never heard of or seen any other farm-owners living in a *rondavel*. Defying convention, my parents used the *rondavel* which remained from the Welstein's time, as a bedroom. It was reached by crossing five or six stepping-stones of cement slabs from the verandah, spanning the perhaps four metres between it and the main building.

Unlike Anna Finster on Kwartel, we had no bathroom. We had a kind of splash bath in a big zinc bathtub placed on the floor of the *rondavel*, filled with hot water from the kettle on the wood stove carried there for this purpose. Even though there was the standard wooden washstand with matching ceramic jug and basin, I do not remember it ever being used. The routine of using the outhouse also differed from Kwartel. No need for fear of scorpions or the odd cobra in the dark of the outhouse this time. Everything was visible and clear. The veld with bushes near to the house was sought for this purpose – or else at night, the potty was placed under one of the beds. My father slept in an extraordinarily high bed, my mother in a lower, smaller one, with my sister or I between them. A wardrobe decorated with engravings held clothes, bedding and other possessions. Mostly in winter a big furry and cosy blanket of several jackal skins sewn together, covered the bed.

Once we had settled on Kwartel Wes after my grandfather's death, a pleasant routine developed and we had some good times there. A tradition with almost religious attributes was our regular Sunday visits to Anna Finster on Kwartel. My favourite uncle, Hans, would come from Tierkolkies, the farm bequeathed to him at the death of my grandfather. We would drive east from Kwartel Wes. In theory, Sunday visits were a chance to discuss farming and financial matters, test the waters about cattle auctions and even politics. Disembarking from our grey Ford pickup, we would greet Anna Finster, sitting on a wicker chair in the shade of the house. She would not always look happy to see us. No doubt this would relate to events of the Sunday before. My mother would normally be sent off to the kitchen to make tea for everybody. Anna Finster, her hair closely tucked under a hairnet, legs crossed under her, would not move from her wicker chair, as my father and uncle would lounge in various postures of relaxation on the verandah steps or casually lean against the house wall. The chatting would be intermittent, punctuated by long silences. Tea would arrive and be drunk in silence. Then the conversation might pick up a little. Soon, however, the tone would change and voices would become raised as the talking became more heated. It usually concerned some affair related to the farm or farming or stock and, of course, the bottom line, money. Hans would usually remain more or less calm, but I could easily detect when my father became agitated. His eyebrows would become furrowed. The corners of his mouth would drop.

It would not take long and my father would become increasingly angry. Hans might throw in a word or two; Anna Finster would slap her thighs and would swear that she definitely had not *"so waar nie ..."*, wag her finger at her two grown sons in a menacing manner, indicating she never would *"nooit nie ..."*, characteristically drawing out the syllable of *"oooii"* and then in a gesture of concluding defiance, fold her arms under her somewhat sagging breasts. As if on cue, my mother would be called from the kitchen where she was washing the teacups. I would be ordered to get up from where I was "playing outside" within earshot of the grownups. We would scramble to the cars and drive off in a huff. We would leave Anna Finster sitting in her chair in the same posture as at our arrival, her delicate profile turned towards a spot somewhere in the distance, a determined expression around her mouth.

Tempers usually cooled over the coming week. For sure, by the arrival of the following Sunday we would once again find ourselves en route to Kwartel. I once asked my father why it was necessary to go to Kwartel every Sunday, if they would only fight anyway. "No, we will just have to go" would be his standard terse reply so characteristic of my father and devoid of any meaning. What he actually meant was: "I feel I should go. Otherwise I might miss out on something."

This uncomplicated and sheltered rural way of life came to an abrupt and painful end when I turned six. It would take me decades, with extensive personal growth and leaving the country, to once again consider Rehoboth and its surroundings as a home of sorts. The changes that came about in 1957 and the following year were related to my schooling and underlying that, to our ethnic identities.

The closer I came to school-going age, the more my parents must have felt the painful quandary. What were they to do with me? Should they send me to school in Rehoboth? Unless things had changed, they would knowingly expose me to the same misplacement and confusion Hedi had endured. Should they start afresh somewhere else? How to go about this? They belonged on the farm. All their security was wound up with the area: their family, the language they spoke, the little capital they possessed. I can imagine that Anna Finster would have added to their dilemma by pressing for me to leave as she had encouraged Hedi to do. Quite obviously, better chances were to be had away from Rehoboth, particularly if one was white. Here fate was in my favour: by the trick of genetics I am endowed with physical features that, to the uninitiated, would seem to be northern European. I inherited my looks from my father's blonde, light-complexioned European side, rather than from my mother's olive-skinned heritage. Not knowing about my ethnic background, nobody would ever suspect me of being anything other than German. As had been the case with Hedi, this was one of the prerequisites for jumping the colour line. It did not mean that anybody with less European features could not have done so, but it would have been more difficult. Looking at it from this point of view, both Hedi and I were blessed. With all of this wishful thinking at the back of her mind, and ever watchful for better chances on the other ethnic side, Hedi had also made sure that even my name – Ursula Marlene – was as German as it could get. And unless one knew Rehoboth, my surname of Dentlinger not only had a pleasant musical ring to it, but was also German from three generations back.

And so, to put a stop to my parent's indecision, Hedi came up with the solution. "I wanted to save you too", is how she put it to me that afternoon in the cool verandah of her Windhoek home. "That is why we took you to Swakopmund to be baptised there, rather than in Rehoboth. After some discussion with your father and mother, we decided that they should come with us to Rhodesia."

Today, I doubt that any discussion actually took place. I can only imagine my parents giving in to her suggestion without debate or consultation, but with much trepidation. They would have felt small and powerless in the face of the laws of the land. Being inherently honest and law-abiding citizens, they would have been aware of embarking on a venture which involved breaking the law. They must have feared the dangers involved in being detected, yet also wanting to live out their ambitions, particularly for me. Finally they must have seen it as the only way out. So, one day we set off in our grey farm Ford with very little luggage and even less knowledge of what awaited us, wherever we were going. Apparently we headed for the then Rhodesia (now Zimbabwe) via Johannesburg. With that decision, my life was going to change forever.

Just as Hedi had been highly pregnant during her flight to Angola, my mother was highly pregnant with my sister in 1957. By leaving the Rehoboth area, the intention had been to have my sister born in Rhodesia, outside any apartheid policy area. Thereby she would have a foreign place of birth entered on her birth certificate. This would be one less factor confining her to the ethnic category of Coloured for the rest of her life, at a time when the racial category of a person was still community orientated.[93] If this plan succeeded she would ultimately be free to shape her life within a wider and better spectrum of possibilities. Hedi would tell me decades later: "We thought we had given your mother enough time, but your sister arrived early – in fact still while in Johannesburg. This was not planned. Together we decided that your father, mother and newborn sister should stay behind, while my family continued on to Rhodesia with you."

Obviously I was not involved in any decision. These were neither times nor matters where consultation with a child was any consideration. I can imagine my mother not having had much of a say in this either. Perhaps she secretly felt guilty for having given birth early. She was probably treated somewhat as handicapped, having just given birth and now having to care for a newborn baby. By then the adults must have been in a flight mode and now had to deal with the first unforeseen obstruction to their plans.

A very clear picture in my memory, though, is that of my mother in her morning gown in the maternity ward of the hospital in Johannesburg. It was 19 December 1957, the first day after the birth of my sister. Everybody was oohing and aahing over the newborn baby. As usual I was left to my own devices. It was only very much later that I realised that this meeting in the hospital had been a farewell of sorts. Following this visit Hedi, Hans, her two children and I were on our way to Rhodesia while my parents remained behind. After six years of an intense, close-knit life with nobody else but my parents, I was now on my own.

I wish I could for the sake of dramatic effect at this point present a litany of woes. I cannot do that. So traumatised was I that I remember little of the following nine months. Even sitting with Hedi recently while she tried to jolt my memory by describing one or the other incident, did not help me recollect much of what happened in the two towns we lived in what is now

Zimbabwe. Of the car trip there I have vague images of small, cheap hotel rooms and the embarrassment of not knowing where the bathroom was and us children being lifted to relieve ourselves in the washbasin.

One pleasant fleeting memory is that of an orchard of rows of fruit trees full of fruit, as yet unknown to us from semi-arid Namibia. This was in the garden behind a house rented in the Zimbabwean town of Gwelo, so Hedi tells me. Then there was a barren front yard we played in. This must have been in our second house in Kwekwe. Mostly I remember excruciating longing for my parents. I remember going outside every morning after breakfast and sitting in this unkempt yard facing the road beyond the buildings, watching each passing car, hoping to see my parents' car. I was determined that they were on their way to fetch me. So, day-in, day-out, I would watch the street. When I would then return to the house, smitten, I was teased by the rest of the family. If there was any understanding or sympathy shown, I don't remember it. In fact, I cannot remember any incident of kindness or affection, a hug, a comforting word extended to me from anybody during this period of time. I would sleepwalk. Of course I did not recollect that either. But Hedi would regularly say to me in the morning: "You again got out your suitcase from under the bed during the night, started packing it and walked around the house."

In later years after I'd had my own children, I often thought of these experiences. I could not help but smile when our sons started kindergarten in Oregon. In this gentle society – certainly gentle in this respect – we, as mothers, were encouraged to remain in class for the initial period. The kindergarten teacher explained that preschool children should be eased into this new arrangement in order not to suffer from separation anxiety. In 1957 in Namibia, adults had not even heard of the psychological effects of separation anxiety, nor was there time to devote to problems of this kind in any case.

Life could not have been very calm and secure in Rhodesia. Even though Hans had found a job, I am sure finances were tight. But even if finances had allowed the occasional phone call home, this would not have been possible. There were no phones on Kwartel Wes or Kwartel. Therefore, during these excruciating nine months, I never once spoke to my parents. Of course I did not understand any of what was happening to me. Nobody had explained anything. At least I do not remember any conversation about how long I was to remain in the country, or about when, where or whether at all my parents were going to fetch me. I simply missed, with a child's innocence, everything that had been my life until then: the farm, ou Lenas, our house, the warmth, the open spaces, and most of all, my parents. All was gone. The yearning became a physical pain. I was too young to have verbalised any of this, but even if I had, I believe nobody would have listened because I was a child. I felt totally abandoned and powerless. I must have learned that nothing could change my situation. My subconscious response was to escape with my clothes at night.[94]

My desperation did not end after my nine months in Rhodesia with Hedi and her family. I believe there to have been some sort of reunion with my parents, which should have meant a release from the agony, but I do not remember any. A more important concern of my parents must have been my timely schooling. I was now seven years old and quite obviously they had to make a decision. Somehow this came to pass. My next distinct image is that of starting school in South Africa, in Cape Town.

In 1958, the German St. Martini School, established in 1883 as a parish school, was at the top of Queen Victoria Street. I have no idea how my registration there even came about. I must have had a passport travelling to Rhodesia. On it, my place of birth, Rehoboth, would have classified me as coloured. This would have forbidden me to attend a white school. But perhaps in those years not too many questions were asked. And since the school had struggled financially for many years, the school board might have been prepared to enrol any "wayward Germans"[95] without too much fuss. For, although we had spoken only Afrikaans and Khoe on the farm, by 1958 we had miraculously switched to German en route to Rhodesia. What an interesting form of German this must have been! We cared neither about declination of nouns, nor conjugation of verbs. But however it sounded, we qualified as German-speaking and I was therefore able to escape any scrutiny of my ethnic origins.

Were all these details of a finely worked out plan? I doubt it. On the whole we were modest, uneducated country folk rather than schemers, but we were smart enough to recognise a good chance when it came our way. Switching our mother tongue to German might simply have been the result of leaving Namibia, as paradoxical as that may sound. Already with her move from Kwartel to Swakopmund, Hedi had started speaking German and continued to do so after her marriage. Hans was of German background and perhaps not fluent in Afrikaans, certainly not in English. For us, to speak German was a good cover in English-speaking Rhodesia, and it seemed obvious to anyone for us to speak German coming from Namibia. In retrospect, the detour via Rhodesia was a clever ploy and consequently eased my immersion into a new environment and role as a white pupil at a German school.

I was, of course, totally oblivious of this fortunate stroke of luck. Psychologically I must have felt my new situation to be a mere continuation of the same desperate desertion I had already experienced in Rhodesia. True to family tradition, no emotions were expressed. No experiences were discussed. With whom was I to discuss my feelings anyway? My parents were back at Kwartel Wes living on the farm. Cape Town needed adapting to. It was yet again different to Gwelo and Kwekwe. It was a coastal town. It became cold in winter. English was the language spoken outside the confines of the school and boarding school. The food, the smells, the people were all foreign to me. I simply could not stomach the high starch diet, having been used to a lot of protein. Mostly though, I felt totally deserted. Each morning before leaving for school from the big old house acting as a boarding school, I would throw up into the flowerbeds the porridge we had just eaten. I had become so nervous that I could not keep it down.

My parents must eventually have realised the disastrous effects the separation had had on me. Or was it the next planned step in our change of ethnic identity? For whatever reason, they decided to come to the Cape. Together with another German-speaking Namibian, a Herr Lisse, they settled in Riebeeck Kasteel, then a village some eighty-five kilometres from Cape Town. I remember a house on a street corner very much in the centre of town, with almond trees in the garden.[96] At least I was now able to see them on the occasional weekend. My father worked in the cement factory at Riebeeck Wes and prided himself on the fact that he learned to speak English by reading the daily English newspaper. However, this arrangement did not last long. He soon returned to Namibia to work on the Cordon, the veterinary fence in eastern, northern and western Namibia, leaving my mother, my sister and me behind. We boarded just two houses down from the boarding school, at 33 Upper Orange Street in Cape Town. Here we lived happily for the year of 1959 in the company of other boarders and our landlady. My mother took to Cape Town like a fish to water. How she did it, I have no idea. She did not speak a word of English, only her broken German. She cleaned in the boarding house and this earned us free lodging. We lived poorly in the former maid's quarters in the damp and dark backyard of the double-storied house with an outside toilet and a bathroom in the main house.

In spite of the material hardship, it was an extremely harmonious, self-contained and protected life for the three of us, and I presume, for the other female boarders as well. The core group of women consisted of my mother, our German landlady *Frau* Girbig, and Ille Rooseboom (nee Seeliger), who would invite us to spend weekends at her spectacularly positioned family home on the beachfront in Kommetjie. The women worked and cooked together, sharing the raising of my sister and me. From these years, a friendship developed that lasted many decades. In the eighties and early nineties, I would return to the Cape with our children from the States and spend time with the two Seeliger sisters at their Kommetjie house, "Lorelei". They became my substitute female relatives, and as children and even later as students, we would spend many happy weekends in Kommetjie. I do believe, however, that my mother's contentment resulted in her drifting away from my father and that from 1959 onwards, their marriage was never again the same.

Living in such close daily proximity, our background could not have remained a secret for long. The elderly ladies must soon have detected the illiteracy of my mother. Within this sisterhood they must have realised that their support was needed. For instance, when I brought home any assign-ment or my biannual report from school to be signed, my mother and the other women in the house must have been in a quandary. Who would sign it? My mother could not do so. Was it legally possible for any of the other women in the house to sign for her? What if the teacher would openly ques-tion the authenticity of the signature in class? They would not have dared risking anything in which I might be publicly exposed. The times and situa-tion required ingenuity. Perhaps one of them spoke to the school principal on our behalf. In the end, my reports were always signed with my mother's name but not by her.

After a year or so, my mother returned to Namibia and the farm, togeth-er with my sister. I would come home twice a year for five weeks over Christmas and for three weeks during the winter vacation only. There were a number of fellow students from Namibia in the school but also in the boarding house, and together, we would take the three-day train trip from Cape Town to Namibia. All in all, this was not an ideal situation to encourage a warm and supportive family life. In fact, I had begun to live a life parallel to that of my parents much earlier than most other children my age. We could no longer relate to each other culturally, linguistically or academically. Still, I continued to have a respectful if not particularly deep relationship with my father. The relationship with my mother, however, was different: until the end of her life and in spite of wide geographical separation and intellec-tual differences, both my sister and I cared deeply for her and loved her with-out question. As I am now of a similar age to hers at the time her death, I can see that it was she who had intuitively set the ground for our relation-ship. It is with deep gratitude and profound satisfaction that I acknowledge that we did not let a political system come in the way of our love for each other.

As the years went on – and being a resilient child – I eventually settled down at the German School in Cape Town and was happy there. If at first our spoken German had been devoid of any proper grammar or syntax, this soon became history. People like Elisabeth Wandres, spinster and superintendent of the boarding school, and Heinrich von Holten, the school principal, were instrumental in upholding German culture here at the tip of Africa. First and foremost this meant the proper command of the German language. Speaking English was not tolerated by Fräulein Wandres, even though the world spoke nothing but English once you stepped out of the front gate.

Sports event at the German School, 1966

I cannot remember any regular visits to Anna Finster on Kwartel during this time. This seems a shame. Presumably, my progress would have pleased my Germanophile grandmother. She could have listened to my perfect German, rejoicing at her vision for her lighter-skinned offspring finally being realised. Not only did we pass as white – but as German! But perhaps the tradition of family secrecy continued, in fact even more so than before. Now that we were white and German, we would not have jeopardised our newly acquired status for anything. In retrospect, this seems to be an immeasurably sad position to have to adopt. There was not going to be any celebration of this supposedly wonderful achievement, no rites of passage as one acquired a new status. Now we carried the fear of detection around with us. We did not exactly avoid contact with family members in Rehoboth, but we did not seek them out either. Perhaps there just was not enough time during my short stay on the farm. At least this is what I remember.

During those years, I was far from proud of our life on Kwartel Wes. In fact, I was embarrassed and humiliated by it. I was ashamed of our poverty: the paraffin stands, the *rondavel* as a bedroom for my parents, the smallness of our home, the aridity and lack of comfort with not even the least bit of luxury or possibility of leisure. Everything was geared towards maximum work. I talked to my father about this. After all, in Cape Town at the German School I had friends who were children of professors. I had become acquainted with middle-class white life.

After some prodding and pushing, my father promised he would build us a new house on Kwartel Wes. I was excited about this prospect. The new house was finally built. It turned out to be a mixed blessing: it was bigger, yes, but it was a prefab house. The outside facade of corrugated iron sheets made the inside just as unbearably hot in summer and ice-cold in winter, as had been the case in the *rondavel*. Also, it was quite clear to me that this type of building material was by far inferior to the brick and mortar homes that I had become accustomed to in Cape Town.

The year of 1963 brought about some important changes in our lives, some of which I have only discovered in 2015, when I found the original marriage certificate of my parents. On the date of their marriage, 25 January 1944, they were entered as *kleurling* or coloured on their marriage certificate under the category 'race' by the hand of Pastor W. Lind, the Rhenish missionary at the time. This, in itself, was no surprise to me. This is how we had always lived our lives. In 1962, though, the Lind classification was revised. Under the rubric *ras* – race, the word *kleurling* – coloured – is unceremoniously deleted by pen, and *blanke* – white – is printed above it and initialled, all in a rather flourished handwriting. This deletion is signed by Pastor J. Beukes. A second entry made in 1963 shows a confirmation of the 1962 change. This time only initialled J.B. This, too, seemed a logical next step in the sequence. Needless to say, what totally confused me was that under a column 'comments' it states that these re-classifications were made on the basis of the original birth certificates of my parents, which obviously had declared them white and not coloured. A date of 23.6.1960 is given for – probably – later issued and abridged birth certificates.

I needed time to understand and take this in. According to this information, my parents were declared white at birth. At their marriage they were classified coloured. In 1962/3 they were once again re-classified white in accordance with their original status1. A comment by my father vaguely came to mind. He had maintained that all Rehobothers born before a year late in the 1920s were automatically declared white. Regarding my mother, the lady in charge of the church records also maintained that, to her knowledge, everyone born in the south of Namibia of mixed heritage was declared white.

After I had caught my breath, I realised how sporadic and changeable legal classifications could be. By the stroke of a pen, our process of jumping the colour line had come to fruition! A lifetime of anguish was declared unnecessary! But the fears would remain.

Once I applied for an identity document, which I needed for travelling back and forth between Namibia and South Africa, I was automatically classified as white according to the law[97] which stated: " 'European' means a person who in appearance obviously is, or who by general acceptance and repute is a European".[98] Since the pastor, my teachers and my neighbours generally accepted me as white and I lived in a white area – I was white!

Being classified as white made it possible for us to leave the Rehoboth area and so, in the winter of 1963, we moved into the white farming community of Seeis, twelve kilometres east of the international airport outside Windhoek. My father kept Kwartel Wes and would return there weekly. I felt more comfortable living in a white area. No more embarrassments about being picked up at Bahnhof outside Rehoboth. No more corrugated iron walls of a house. Our neighbours spoke German. My mother, too, felt at home in the Seeis area. But I always felt that my father had deep-seated issues with acceptance, even though he seemed to be respected by the community as a good farmer. He would ultimately return to the Rehoboth area.

In the meantime in Cape Town, classes were moved from the former St. Martini School to a new area on the slopes of Signal Hill in 1963. It was known to be one of the most beautifully situated schools in the world with its sweeping view of the whole of Cape Town and Table Bay at its feet. Over the years, I settled into the new routine of being a student in Cape Town, and was more relaxed about my background since we had moved to the Windhoek area.

From the outside, I seemed to be coping quite well. Not only did I become a relatively good sportswoman, but also a good scholar. I was reasonably popular and took part in all the normal activities of teenagers such as having boyfriends, going out and having several close girlfriends. However, in spite of my appearance as a fun-loving, successful and popular high school

With my father at Seeis, December 1984

student, I had a silent layer of vulnerability, a pronounced seriousness and oversensitivity hidden under the surface. Although it may not have been evident to others, I carried it around with me constantly. If, for instance, I produced a piece of work that was not up to my usual standard, instead of putting it behind me and moving on, I would dwell on it longer than was necessary or good for me. It seemed as if I began to take every adversity more seriously than was called for. I castigated myself silently, more harshly than my fellow students did.

It was during adolescence that this fearfulness and doubt about my person and my abilities became ever more strong. It was a strange sensation. Even though I excelled in much of what I did, I would diminish these accomplishments, argue them away in my mind. I cannot pinpoint the exact moment at which I connected this behaviour to my background. There must have been a time when I asked myself: how can you ever be confident, when you secretly know you come from a section of society that the world considers inferior? How can you ever truly be able to reach their standards? I experienced these questions not as words, but as feelings, subconscious sensations. Then, I had not yet learned to verbalise what was going on inside me. Sadly, that only happened years later.

In retrospect, I believe that harsh self-criticism can become part of any young adolescent grappling with the question of identity. Admittedly though, I had more on my psychological plate than the average teenager. At university, we discovered and discussed how children who grow up in institutions develop differently to those from a sheltered, supportive family environment, appearing to mature earlier but often lacking in self-esteem. Such factors must have influenced the shaping of my young, often brittle personality. Sadly though, I also had to contend with the more weighty and secret issue of our ethnicity. A love affair would break up, and somewhere in the recesses of my mind the question would appear: was this related to where I came from? Could it possibly be that the young man, or perhaps his parents even, saw a problem in my mixed background? At times I almost wished adversity along, pre-empting it. For instance, I had not learned to read a map. "Well, we never learned to read maps in the Basterland", an inner voice would explain. The voice would be apologetic, submissive, self-reproaching. Zoe Wicomb talks of a "consciousness of inferiority"[99], which is an apt description of the feelings of general inadequacy and questioning of self-worth I experienced.

Today I understand that we could not have done differently. Our secret background had clouded our perceptions of ourselves and the world around us. Just like the middle-class white society we had become part of, we too had come to internalise the message that brown was NOT beautiful, brown was inferior - in fact, it was shameful. Therefore, dodge, run and hide when

*My father and
Robert at Seeis,
1988*

the question "where are you from" comes up! Be on guard at all times! Don't give yourself away - fit in and blend!

This awareness of living a double life took up a lot of energy. We felt separate from the rest of the world in a mysterious kind of way. As Hedi had experienced, it was lonely in the sense of not being able to open up and admit our background. Had we done so, I believe it could have been a shared and consequently a lighter burden. In my younger years, we should have discussed all of these issues with the sympathetic ladies in our circle in Upper Orange Street. But for some reason this never happened. Perhaps everybody felt I was too young. Perhaps they were put off from probing deeper by the despair my mother exuded when confronted with anything remotely associated with her background. From the start, our family tradition of secrecy prevented any doors being opened.

Another inhibiting factor was geography. Our family was split up most of the time. My sister attended two German schools in Windhoek, while I received all my schooling in Cape Town, both of us away from the farm. So there was no strength in numbers; everything remained hidden, latent, unspoken. There were no conversations around the dinner table in the even-

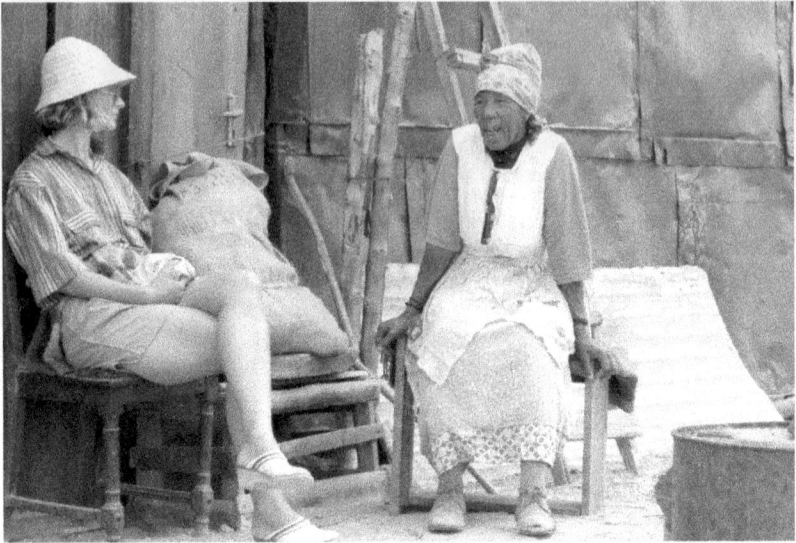

Johanna Fischer and myself at Sout Rivier on the Kuiseb River, January 1985

ing where we could all let off steam. After an injustice faced or disappoint-ment felt during the day, there was nobody to comfort with "I love you any-way" or more assertively "to hell with that" or "who cares?" There was never a chance to suggest, "Why don't we simply come out, leave the racial closet?" or to say, "Let's just see what that will bring." Spatial separation had restricted our family interaction to rare occasions. When we were together, there seemed little time or inclination to talk about our background.

These are complex psychological issues, hard to analyse in retrospect. The paradox of the situation was that nobody from the outside ever demand-ed an explanation for our heritage. Occasionally fellow students teased me about my background. If they knew about Rehoboth, they might call me a Baster. Of course, I panicked. It was painful. However, this is as far as it ever went. Today I believe that this was not different to a student being teased about protruding ears, a weight problem or being called a nerd. Being teased is part of adolescent life. In fact, one might argue it is a form of acceptance. My greatest fear was of being asked where my mother went to school, did she study or the same about my father. But they were never really asked in any insistent manner, only in passing. Nobody ever scrutinised or interrogat-ed me about my background. I was lucky not to have been told on the way Hedi was in Swakopmund. On the contrary, I had a wide circle of lovely friends. This truly was a wonderful support and I believe that they helped tremendously. Even today I still have a strong bond with many of my girl-friends from school and we see each other whenever time allows. I had two wonderful young male friends at school, boyfriends. One, in particular, I had a friendship with enduring many years. His support and love shaped my later life.[100] The comment of my Afrikaans teacher, Marie Smit, probably best sums up the approach of people around me: *"ons het geweet, maar nie getraak nie"* – we knew but did not care. These were all positive messages that must have hit a certain deep psychological mark somewhere in my being.

We did well for ourselves; we played our adopted roles well. Nobody suspected the anguish lying hidden below the surface. None of us became suicidal or turned to drink or went on a shooting rampage. This was the ultimate paradox: we were good at almost everything, even assimilation into white culture. We did so well that my cousin Harold, who had remained in Namibia and Rehoboth, told me recently that he believed our life "playing in the light"[101] and living in white society had been a pleasure, success, a walk in the park. He was surprised to hear the opposite.

Perhaps because my early childhood had been wonderfully sheltered and loving, and my adolescence successful and gregarious in spite of my ethnic hang-ups, I was able to eventually accept my ethnic background openly. Already as a young student I was immensely intrigued by any "otherness" in people. Secretly, I hoped to find answers to my own background in anthropology. Thus, I remained drawn to the farms of my childhood, even though I might have been happy not to be living there anymore.

Lately these are my thoughts as I drive the B1 from Windhoek to Rehoboth, which I do on a regular basis, past the new lodges, the poor homesteads and the deserted petrol station. I no longer cringe, as I did as a child when my parents picked me up from the train station Bahnhof, coming on holiday from the white German school in Cape Town.

It seems a shame that it took so long for us to see the benefits of the mixed heritage we had. We could have let go of our fears earlier, but instead we clung to them. At my assumed wise age of sixty-three, I now regret that we did not show more courage. But I'm happy to say that now, finally, I like my mixed background. I no longer need to prove anything to anybody. In fact, I would not want to exchange my multi-ethnic background for any other. With the hindsight and experience of the years, I believe we overreacted. I now believe that people were much more tolerant than we anticipated. In fact, on the whole, people were accepting, gentle and kind. Instead of cowering, we should have stood up for our background.

Family members deal with family issues differently. Ou Lenas, more than anybody else I know, lived her life to the fullest. In spite of being positioned at the very bottom of the racial pyramid, she came to full bloom there and then. She simply ignored ethnicity and colour. Hedi instinctively understood ethnicity and the way it worked. Until today she continues believing in the cultural and material superiority of one ethnic group above that of another. She struggled to change her ethnic belonging to the group that would give her better chances and a higher status. I wrestled with it. From early on, I was deeply influenced by individuals close to me coming from opposing cultures. I believe I had incorporated a certain cultural relativity. Yet, society around me was demanding and legalising cultural and ethnic inequality and, in fact, grading. Thus, it took me many years and extensive research and travel, comparing other countries to Namibia and South Africa, to justify my latent tendencies.

Curiously, my mother's family, the Enssles, approached the issue of ethnicity from yet another perspective. For reasons of their own, they simply stayed put in their ethnic environment. Remaining in the wider Rehoboth area they rode the waves of history and the changes of the times. Once apartheid was abolished in Namibia in 1990, they were free, just like us, and equal before the law and did as they pleased. They exploited chances available and did not fare badly. More importantly, they did not have to make the sacrifices that Hedi and I had made.

6 THE ENSSLES AND THE DENTLINGERS

Mixed marriages can be a mixed blessing. The mixed marriages of our fore-fathers brought us political and social prejudice, family disconnection and psychological pain. Hedi suffered at the hands of a colour-based political system which she fought until she attained her personal goals. I initially suf-fered as well, forced to deal with it according to my own devices. Other relatives who remained behind in Namibia would have choices denied, opportunities thwarted. It is only once the discriminatory system was removed that we could breathe more freely. Now that we have the ability and freedom to move even further, beyond prejudice or to learn to ignore it, it is possible to appreciate the gift of cultural wealth that a mixed heritage brings with it.

No doubt our forefathers did not dream that their choice of marriage partner would one day force their descendants to wrestle with a burden of their making. But wrestle we did, though each in our different ways.

My mother's family, the Enssles, took yet another approach. I was to get an insight into their stance on mixed marriages. Five years ago, one leisure-ly evening a group of us were sitting in a restaurant in Windhoek. My cousin Alma and her husband were there with their mother Louisa, one of my moth-er's siblings. The talk revolved around life on Gamis where all the Enssle sib-lings had grown up. Louisa was entertaining us with stories about their tra-ditions and way of life during the 1940s.

"On the farm, everybody had their chores. The two-roomed house was small and the family big," Louisa told us. "We tended to the sheep and goats in the morning, milked the ewes and separated the lambs from their moth-ers before they were driven out for grazing." After this, the girls would come home to fetch water, keep the house in order, do the laundry for the family as a whole, collect wood and help with the cooking. Only then would they wash and change into clean clothes.

As each of the Enssle girls reached marrying age and young men came to court, they would take particular care with their appearance. Louisa assured us that, as the ultimate proof of good breeding, it was a prerequisite that the dress they wore with the collar buttoned up, did not show any fray-ing at the elbows.

Courting was a serious business. "A young man might be told by his mother to go and visit one or other farm, where he could later choose a wife," Louisa told us. "Ideally this process would have to be carried out in a particular way. He would travel from farm to farm by bicycle or horse cart. Donkey carts were considered to be of lesser status. On Gamis, the arrival of the young man would be visible for miles over the flat plains, long before he arrived. We girls would, of course, know who the young man approaching was. He had to appear *amptelik, met baaitjie en das* - official, in jacket and tie. Sometimes he would wear a *stofdas* - a coat of sorts against the dust.

"Once he had pulled up at the house, some good chairs were brought out for the prospective wooers to sit on. But this was always a problem for us. Usually there were no more than two respectable chairs. We were poor. The chairs would then ceremoniously be placed on the *kleitjie* - a mat of tanned goat skin cut into pieces and sewn together placing colours in an alternating pattern much like a checkerboard, with a white fur edging. And then the important business of courting could start ..."[102]

The Enssles are known for their humour and light-heartedness. In true Enssle fashion, even before Louisa had finished, she was interrupted with disbelief, teased and the details of her story made fun of.

"But how can you call that courting?" someone had asked. It was difficult to believe under modern circumstances. "These young men came ... to sit with you on the *vel* in the *vlakte* -on the tanned hide in the desert?"

She remained unperturbed. "Oh, they came from far, Rehoboth, other farms."

"From Rehoboth? A hundred and twenty kilometres in a cart ... to sit on the vel with you to talk?" The young people found it hard to believe the amount of effort undertaken for so small a reward.

Even though the atmosphere soon became somewhat raucous with merriment, Louisa remained calm and assertive about her story, maintaining that courting was a serious business. "You had to marry *half-slag* - someone of mixed ethnic background." She repeated the well-known sentiment of the day: "The lighter, the better." And then almost as an afterthought: "*Dit is mos net die blankes wat iets getel het* - it's only the whites who mattered."

This is how my father must have ridden over the plains of Gamis to court my mother, in this proper and serious manner. Anna Finster, my father's headstrong mother, had made up her mind that her most European-looking son should "marry up". For Anna Finster, this meant not only as white as possible, but, true to her pro-German sentiments, as German as possible. She must somewhere have heard about the Enssle girls on Gamis with their German father and respectable mixed-background mother. From that moment onwards, my father would have had no other chance. Hedi confirms that Anna Finster herself had come to Gamis once to start the marriage negotiations.[103] After the first visit, she then sent my father to go to visit there and "have a look".[104]

Intrigued by this almost-arranged kind of marriage, I was able to ask my father about it before he died in 2001. He agreed it was all true. I asked him, "Well, did you marry my mother because your mother told you to?" He answered, as evasive as ever, "I did go and visit there and enjoyed it - and so the friendship developed." The relationship between my parents had become strained in later years.

"Well, did you love her then?" I had to know.

This he answered honestly, I think, with: "Yes ... at the beginning ..."

Nevertheless, they were married on Kwartel on 25 January 1944 and made a dashing couple at the time.

Even though my parents made a perfect match from the point of view of ethnic background, marrying "up" was not what my German male forefathers did. According to the value system of the day, they married decidedly "down".

In January 1905, my maternal grandfather, Albert Enssle, entered Namibia at Lüderitz Bay on the ship *Wittekind*. He had given his last address in Germany as Donau-Eschingen.[105] Family tradition has it that he joined the *Schutztruppe* - the German colonial military forces - as a saddle-repairer and not as a soldier. Later official archival documents during the times of South African mandateship refer to him as an employee of Alfred Breiting of Gamis, with his occupation as being a general farm assistant or a carpenter/blacksmith. It is hard to connect his employment to a particular date.

Family reminiscences tell that Albert Enssle and Susanna Bezuidenhout met in Bethanie. This must have taken place during the early 1920s, as the second set of twins, Jakob and Hans, were born in 1923. This is where my mother was born in 1927, and a brother, Albert, a little later. By the time they settled on Gamis, the number of children totalled four. The next three followed in close succession: twins Elisabeth and Mariechen in 1935, and Louisa in 1937. All in all there were three sets of twins in the family, though the first set died early.

Apart from Louisa's stories about courting practices of the day, I often try to visualise life on Gamis. It must have been unusual in many ways, to say the least. My mother described her father as a very "correct" man. From the only photograph that has remained, one can tell very little about Albert Enssle. It is a posed, typically nineteenth century passport-type photograph showing a stern man with a high forehead and (for those days) a fashionable, thin moustache and round spectacles. Personally, I suspect that "correct" was a euphemism for "authoritarian and distant". He liked onions, she would recall. Once, when we visited Gamis with the Enssle siblings, they stood at the house, recalling how their father would walk back from work slowly, bowed over, at the end of the day. He seems not to have been a healthy man.

How did he communicate with his wife and children? My surviving aunts tell me that they would speak Afrikaans and Khoe at home, both languages that were unknown to Albert Enssle. It was only Jakob, the oldest son, who spoke a fair amount of German as he had worked for German employers

My grandmother, Susanna Bezuidenhout, holding my mother, Wilhelmine Enssle, and Hans and Jakob Enssle standing, late 1927

most of his life. The girls never learned German, even though Louisa had worked in a German hotel for many years prior to her marriage. My mother's German was the typical Namibian German often heard, lacking a wide vocabulary and basic structure. How, then, did Albert Enssle communicate with his very African family?

I need to stress again that my family was not literary. Nobody left behind letters or diaries. Also my three remaining aunts are not keen to relate family details, especially not those which are slightly controversial. One rare story told by my uncle, Jakob, tells how Albert Enssle came to settle on Gamis.

He was riding in the south of Namibia together with his friend and *Kamerad* – comrade – Bart, another ex-German soldier. The two must have known each other from before this event. It appeared they were on no particular errand, basically just looking for work. They came close to the farm Gamis, owned by another ex-Schutztruppler named Wede. They saddled off under the tree and decided to lie in wait for Wede. The intention was to shoot the unfortunate man once he came into view, the reason being that he had taken a Rehoboth woman of mixed background for a wife. Obviously this offended Enssle and Bart at the time. This was rather unfair towards Wede,

Mariechen and Tina at Rietoog

because by all accounts he had been more than protective of his wife and children.[106]

Luckily Wede escaped the ill-intended murder by Enssle and Bart, who wisely changed their minds and must have gone along their way. Unfortunately, though, Wede was not so lucky in financial matters. Some years later he hit on bad times and had to declare total bankruptcy.

The interesting conclusion to these events is joyfully told by the present owner of Gamis, Alfred Breiting. He tells how initially Wede had asked his father, Albert Breiting, to stand surety for him in the event of financial difficulties. These German ex-soldiers had also known and obviously trusted each other. This process came to fruition when Wede had to declare bankruptcy. Consequently on 3 July 1923, Albert Breiting suddenly found himself in possession of the farm Gamis. He was now forced to remain in Namibia even though his intentions had been to settle elsewhere.[107]

The irony of fate continues however, for in 1934 Albert Enssle had to appeal to Breiting's generosity. Experiencing hard times, Enssle had wandered around, finding the odd job here and there, but nothing permanent. Finally, he came to Gamis where he was forced to ask Albert Breiting for work. Again Alfred, the son of the original owner Albert Breiting, enjoys relating how his father told Enssle: "You can work for me, but I cannot pay you." Albert Enssle appears to have had no alternative. So a little house was built for him on Gamis. It still stands today, having recently been renovated. He moved into it in 1934 and worked and lived there until the end of his life.

In 1940 he became ill and was taken to hospital in Windhoek, where he died in the same year. The Breitings organised a funeral for him as well as a tombstone, on which two dates are engraved: simply the year of his birth and that of his death. Much later, both my mother's and my sister's ashes were interned into the same grave.

The irony of the family anecdote does not end there, for Albert Enssle moved into the little two-roomed house with his own companion - of mixed background - and their first two children. In the meantime, his friend Bart had also married a Rehoboth woman, and the Bart family has been resident there for many decades since. Apparently the initial indignation the two men had felt towards Wede, an antipathy so strong that they wanted to murder him, was no more. They had radically changed their minds, both choosing partners of mixed heritage.

If the story of Bart and Enssle's bloodthirsty intentions is true, the question arises regarding the opinion of mixed marriages at the time. I would like to assume this incident happened when Albert Enssle had come fresh from Germany during the early 1900s. If so, their opposition to mixed marriages occurred around the time when mixed marriages were looked upon with extreme prejudice by the German colonial administration. Such marriages were forbidden from 23 September 1905 by the decree of acting Governor Hans Tecklenburg, in spite of having been legal in the motherland according to the Consular Act of 1 June, 1870.[108] Obviously there was much opposition from many German men, including Wede, to the treatment of their families and categorisation of their children as natives by the administration.

It is not clear whether Albert Enssle officially married Susanna Bezuidenhout. Was this because of poverty? Or perhaps he feared the law, which by now was South African and equally discriminatory towards mixed marriages. The fact remains that my grandmother retained her maiden name until her death, while all of the children went by their father's surname. Whatever the reasons might be for their relationship to have remained a common-law one, they remained together until Albert's death.[109]

My female Enssle relatives always stress the poverty they grew up under. Albert Enssle's final liquidation and distribution account in 1940[110] listed:

- 201 karakul sheep valued at £200.00
- one ox wagon £25.00
- one set of blacksmith and carpenter tools £25.00
- one Mauser rifle and 15 cartridges[111] £3.00

His total movable property amounted to £254.10 from which had been deducted a dentist bill of £1.00 for a treatment undergone in May 1938.

The distribution record further listed Susanna Bezuidenhout as having been Enssle's cohabitor for nineteen years. She left a mark, but no signature.

A letter written later by attorneys on her behalf requested that the sheep not be sold, since they were needed to pay for school fees for the children. It further requested that her two older sons pay twenty-five pounds upfront to stop the sheep from being sold. This is an indication of the degree of poverty that must have been part of their lives.[112]

This then is the mixed marriage history on my mother's side, the Enssle family. Now I turn to some aspects of the mixed marriage family saga on my father's side, that of Gustav Dentlinger, who married a woman of mixed ethnic background.

As I've mentioned earlier, Hedi tells that in 1892 her grandfather left his native Irslingen in Württemberg together with two friends, a Herr Hummel and a Herr Pegel. Even though I have not been able to find any evidence of this in the most obvious military records, I have reason to believe that Gustav Dentlinger, my great-grandfather and Hedi's grandfather, may have sailed to the *Schutzgebiet* with the 1893 consignment of German soldiers. If the three men boarded the boat at the end of 1892, it could have taken them until March 1893 to arrive at Walvis Bay. Alternatively, they might have taken a different route, namely via the Cape.[113] A cursory search in the archives in Cape Town unfortunately did not confirm this.[114]

Hedi further relates that in Bethanie, Dentlinger met and married her grandmother, Sabina Olivier. We assume she was of mixed Dutch slave origin as is suggested by her name; her father perhaps from the Dutch settlers at the Cape, her mother of slave origin. With that racial combination, apparently she was a striking beauty with long pitch-black silky hair, which she wore plaited down her back. He married her legally and officially in the mission church in Bethanie on 4 March 1896.

Even though I could not verify Sabina's place of origin, the marriage is mentioned in connection with the *Schutztruppe* in colonial documents. An officer, von Burgsdorff, notes in a report on 17 March 1897 that six whites, one of whom was Dentlinger, had married Grootfonteiners.[115] He could not refrain from expressing his opinion about the "mainly negative impact" of mixed marriages between retired soldiers and Baster women on the colony.[116] This antipathy towards mixed marriages was to escalate as time went on.

Again, if these dates are correct - and I have no reason to believe they are not - Gustav Dentlinger must have originally signed up as a soldier in the *Schutztruppe*, deciding to leave it within three years. Not only did he leave the *Schutztruppe*,[117] but he was moved to find a marriage partner from the local community. The question of whether Gustav Dentlinger fought Witbooi at Hoornkrans in 1893 is particularly interesting to me. Would not a young German recruit feel conflict in having to shoot and kill local people, and then four years later marry a member of such a group? German soldiers must have arrived with fairly negative preconceived ideas about Africans. Some changed their opinion surprisingly rapidly, as we have seen. However, Gustav Dentlinger remains of great interest for my family, even though the reasons for this interest differ. I will return to this theme a little later, and also to the Enssles. But now I want to sketch a picture of the man and his financial affairs.

Although there is a dearth of evidence regarding his arrival in the German protectorate and his marriage, ample documents in the National Archives of Namibia in Windhoek give insight into Dentlinger's activities as an entrepreneur. These documents also raise questions about his entrepreneurial abilities, and about the kind of man he was. Family lore and archival evidence agree that on 6 October 1904 he opened and ran a *Handelsgeschäft* – a trading company – in Bethanie in the south of Namibia, with fifteen thousand German marks, a considerable sum of startup capital.[118]

Five months later[119] he wrote to the *Kaiserliches Bezirksgericht* of Keetmanshoop that he wanted to register a partner, a gentleman by the name of Emil Tempel.[120] This re-registration required extensive bureaucratic steps with announcements in the *Hamburger Nachrichten* in Hamburg. By now the capital of the company[121] amounted to one hundred thousand German marks, as he proudly recorded in a letter of 6 November, 1906.

So much more the surprise that less than two years later, on 11 February 1907, the company declared bankruptcy and had to be dissolved. Gustav Dentlinger transferred all his remaining assets to Emil Tempel and was forced to auction off all his possessions.[122] His movable assets on 22 January 1910 were pathetic compared to his original capital. The final distribution list comprised:

- goats worth £400.00
- some chickens and a cockerel
- spoons, 2 water vessels, cups, knives with spoons, £5.00
- worn suits and other items, £15.00
- The total of which amounted to £483,20.[123]

The auction of his immovable assets was held on 8 December 1910.[124] In a letter written at Rehoboth and addressed to the *Kaiserliches Bezirksgericht* at Lüderitzbucht, he had to admit: "*Mein Vermögen* [my assets] ... have all been force-auctioned off and sold. Thus I now own nothing any more".[125]

Already before the final conclusion of these tragic events, Gustav and Sabina must have moved to Rehoboth.[126] I assume that he moved there shortly after the dissolution of the company and became submerged in Rehoboth society, as did so many others seeking refuge. Perhaps he lived the life of a farmer; perhaps he rented land. Here again I can only depend on family history, which states that at some point, he and his son (Hedi's father, my grandfather) Hendrik, worked for the Oliviers, who were said to have been of substance. The next date I could find was the purchase of Kwartel in 1940s by my grandfather.

When I present the archival version of my grandfather's life to family members, they receive it with scepticism and disbelief. They much prefer the successful story of Gustav Dentlinger. They argue for it. For instance, an elderly male relative from Rehoboth maintains that one can still see the name written on the building that once was "his hotel". When I, in turn, argue that this must be extremely durable paint to still be visible after more than a hundred years, he tells me he has nonetheless seen it. I find it endearing that living family members prefer the success version of Gustav Dentlinger. The obvious question is why. I think the obvious answer must be that people like a success story. But over and above that, I wonder if my family prefers it because he was white – and German – and therefore must have been successful? Is this a modern remnant of the sentiments held by Anna Finster in the forties and fifties?

In a way, I, too, am guilty of romanticising my early male ancestor. But I have different reasons for doing so. For one, I believe he must have been quite a character. He is said to have never lost his Swabian dialect, nor a certain quality of life. He was known for his entertaining, and for his humorous and generous manner.[127] His general store in Bethanie was popular, but even more so was his inn. He had also built a bowling alley, which he protected from the dry winds and sand with mats suspended alongside. Soldiers, traders, servants and travellers would stop by, drink his English whisky imported from the Cape, and spin their yarns.[128]

Another aspect of Gustav Dentlinger that intrigues me is the fact that he was one of the first four German ex-soldiers to have openly and officially married a local woman. Just as in South Africa, many young German men would take partners from the indigenous community; these unions were largely ignored by the authorities. But a small number had the courage to marry. No other group of people was more consistently subjected to assessment and surveillance by the state than family members of mixed marriages.

At first, social and administrative discrimination came in the form of loss of jobs or membership of organisations, and prohibition of attendance of children to schools. Later the punitive measures took the form of withdrawal of voting rights, denial of any rights to the women and children, being declared "indigenes".[129] Gustav Dentlinger had the courage to marry his Sabina under circumstances of such extreme discrimination. Hypothetically, he may have married her because her family was apparently relatively wealthy. In my soul, though, I want Gustav Dentlinger to have married Sabina Olivier not for ulterior motives, but from choice; best that he married her out of love. I would like him to have been ahead of his time, free of prejudice, not

concerned about the foreign blood that was going to upset his German genealogy. I hope this was the kind of man that he was. Again, my elderly
Rehoboth relative informs me that he died a violent death. He was shot at
Doornboom, the Olivier farm, "by the Germans". When I asked why, he said,
"because he had opposed them ... Somebody worked to give him a decent
grave". He claims to know the spot. I could not wish for a more exemplary
great-grandfather.

So, Rehoboth became a haven, a refuge for people of all kinds, but particularly for individuals of mixed heritage. Both my families eventually
moved there, the Dentlingers before the Enssles. I would like to conclude this
chapter by returning to the Enssles and exploring the history of the later
generations, before I focus on my mother's life.

Following Albert Enssle's death in 1940, the family continued living on
Gamis for another four years. Thereafter, my grandmother Susanna moved
to Rehoboth with her new partner, and remained there until her death in May
1980. I remember visiting her at her home once, together with my mother.
She had the pronounced Khoe physical features of high cheekbones and
olive-coloured skin. She was gentle and generous, warm and attentive. On
that occasion she gave me an earthenware dish, which since then has held a
special place in my kitchen, holding utensils of daily use. She is buried in the
cemetery in Rehoboth, and I am happy for my mother that she felt free to
visit on numerous occasions while we were living on Seeis, and then finally
to attend her funeral.

Jakob Enssle became employed and remained on Gamis for many years.
I understand from the Breitings that Jakob and his twin brother Hans, had
tried their hand at farming. The two brothers had rented seven hundred hectares at Nomtsas, following some financial assistance from the Breitings.
They acquired some cattle and goats. At first they only farmed over weekends. Much later, however, they resigned from their individual jobs and
moved there permanently to farm. Nomtsas is close to the two farms, Verlos
and Namtses, where we had temporarily lived during my childhood and
where I was given the first of the only two hidings I ever received from my
father. Finally Jakob also came to Rehoboth, where he died in 2012.

Albert Enssle, born on Gamis after my mother in 1939, sadly committed
suicide, having suffered from long-term depression. One of his granddaughters is a medical doctor in Kimberley, in the Cape. His remaining daughters
live in Windhoek and have done particularly well for themselves. Mariechen
(born in 1935) married into the Johrs, another well-known mixed-background
Rehoboth family. They continued living and farming in the area of Gamis, and
I remember visiting her when I was a child. Still today, I can visualise the
aridity of the farm she lived on. And even though we were all poor, hers was
a particularly trying poverty, in a very hot area. She was always sickly and

died early. I recently met her husband, who has since remarried. His new wife is lucky in comparison to Mariechen, in that he has since come to some money and is busy renovating and extending the old house to a notable size. The homestead as a whole now looks far less desolate than it did in my memory.

Another typical Enssle scenario was that of Hans and Tina Enssle (nee Britz). They married at Schlip, east of Gamis, on 12 December 1958. The missionary who married them was Pastor Vollmer, who had also married Ou Lenas in 1936. Tina, by now a widow, relates that there was no church at the time, only a classroom. Predictably, they went to Gamis following their marriage and stayed there for eight years. After that they moved to Rietoog, another farm where Hans became a foreman. Since Rietoog had no school to send their children to, they moved north to Karibib where Hans worked at the local marble-crushing plant for seventeen years, as Hedi's Hans had done. After Hans died in Karibib, Tina came to live in Rehoboth. She has two sons, Hans and Walter. Walter is a teacher, once at Hentiesbaai, now in the south of Namibia. One of her granddaughters is studying engineering in South Africa. On the whole, the different Enssle families ended up successfully.

When I visit Rehoboth, my base is the home of the Benades. Practically the whole family is involved in the running of the local Spar grocery store. Elisabeth Benade (nee Enssle) is the younger sister of my mother. Her kitchen is like a railway station. Employees come and go, perhaps having been sent on some or other errand. Grandchildren drop in after school to say hello to their grandparents. Friends come by to deliver odd items, talk about events in the town. All are offered a cup of tea, and they sit drinking it at the round kitchen table or else on the verandah which also serves as entrance to the kitchen. The door bangs as if in tune with the hustle and bustle flowing through it. The phone keeps ringing. The atmosphere is very different to the somewhat lonely, isolated home of Hedi in Windhoek. Quite clearly the Benades belong to and are part of the community of Rehoboth. It is evidence of a long history of family relations in the area. We phone each other on a regular basis, wherever I might be at the time. I can arrive at their doorstep at the drop of a hat and will always be given a bed and a warm meal.

However, of all Enssle siblings the one I obviously know best is my mother, Wilhelmine. She lived a courageous life and suffered a tragic death. She deserved more recognition, attention, acknowledgement and love than she received. If life were fair, she would have had it easier. One burden she bore – the weight and depth of which even my sister and I could not quite fathom – was that she was illiterate and remained so the whole of her life. I cannot tell how many times I have had to stop in my tracks or lean back in my chair and contemplate this aspect of my mother's fate. How could this have happened? Was it a result of poverty? Or was it neglect? Was it the way of the times? Was it yet another disadvantage of not belonging to the dominant part of society, of being considered ethnically inferior?

Her older brother, Jakob, would relate that there had been no farm school on Gamis then. He would drive the two youngest girls, Liesbeth and Louisa, to school in Schlip or Rietoog, for a while. This seems not to have lasted long, but both girls at least learned the rudimentary elements of spelling and writing. My mother always said that the "old people" expected the children to work around the house. This was true if you were a girl, particularly if you were the firstborn girl. You then had to help raise the younger siblings. This was her explanation for not attending school.

My thoughts return to the relationships within the family, schooling and life in general on Gamis. I am told that little German was spoken in the home. This surprised me, because my mother felt very confident in speaking it when we lived in Upper Orange Street. On Gamis most communication must have been in Afrikaans, and of course everybody, excluding my German grandfather, spoke Khoe. I asked how they had all learned the language.

Elisabeth, referring to her younger years, told me: "Nobody went to school. We played together, the Khoe children and us. Their parents were also our parents. We kids were all treated equally. If one of us had done something wrong, we all got a hiding, either from the Khoe parents or from our own. Nobody felt badly treated. After the group hiding, we would simply continue playing together. This is how we learned to speak Khoe."[130]

Sadly my mother remained illiterate until the day she died. I had realised the dilemma long ago as a young child at the German School in Cape Town, in connection with signing my report. But this was only one of many difficult situations that would face us. When we were teenagers, my sister and I tried to teach her the basics of reading and writing. It was a hard process.[131] She felt incompetent and lacked self-esteem when it came to literacy, even though she was sharp in many other facets of life. She felt most confident when moving and doing things, not sitting and writing.

We finally managed to get her to sign her name. I remember many instances when she would have to sign documents such as bank account applications. We would practise with her long into the night. Even holding a pencil or pen was a totally unfamiliar activity for her, whose hands had always only known manual work. Slowly and concentratedly, she would form each letter. When finally we had to go to bed, we would just hope and pray that the next day, when she had to sign, there would be no queue behind us with customers in a hurry, or that we would find a sympathetic bank attendant. This was during the sixties and seventies, when banking and other official matters were often subject to an employee's discretion. Mostly, the respective attendant would quickly sense that there was a problem, wait patiently and then continue with the processing of the documentation. Sometimes there would be a letter missing in her signature. I don´t think she always noticed herself. Then the bank attendant would just look at it and pass it over. We were lucky once again. In this way, many people understood and helped.

My sister and I would be mortified. I don't believe we were embarrassed for ourselves. No, somehow we had grown to accept her illiteracy, just as we had learned to accept other curious aspects of our family life. But we felt mortified and humbled that she had to go through this ordeal. We felt for her. However, she managed to lend grace to such a situation, showing the utmost seriousness and calm, treating it as a task to be handled with as much care as she could muster. She did not seem nervous or embarrassed; she was almost dignified, certainly unflustered.

She easily picked up the sound of new words, committing them to memory with the intention of using them later. But with only an acoustic reference rather than a visual one, she would sometimes get words mixed up. Later, when living on Seeis, she might receive German-speaking visitors and quite happily tell them: *"Bitte hängen Sie doch Ihren Hut an die Katastrophe."* Please, just leave your hat on the catastrophe.

I have to give our neighbours in the area credit for their understanding and kindness over the years. They must have seen the humour in the situation in the same way as my sister and I did, but kept straight faces nonetheless. Much later and away from my mother, we would use her incorrect phrases just between us, for pure enjoyment. Probably this was our way to deal with an extremely difficult situation, finding a release from the tension of humiliation. At the time though, we would cringe at the awkwardness of her mistakes, feeling for her. Again, however, she would bear herself with grace and without any sign of embarrassment.

Obviously, I cannot and will not try to be objective about her, but most other people who knew her, spontaneously liked her. They considered her to be warm, soft-spoken, generous, hard-working, humble, intelligent, empathetic. My sister and I knew all of that. And she was completely anti-authoritarian, bringing us up in a naturally egalitarian manner. Nothing was too much trouble for her when it involved us. Like most Enssle women, she was a lot of good fun. She was easy to be with, joyful, laughing spontaneously, easily and frequently.

She was also in the forefront of our process of jumping the colour line. Since she was the mother, it was she who stayed with us in Cape Town. In later years when we were teenagers, my father chose to be absent from our lives, very much staying in the background. It was my mother who would come and joyfully visit us in the Cape, at university, with our friends, with our boyfriends of the moment. She twice came to visit when we lived in the

States. She was always directly and deeply connected in our lives. She must have felt awkward, embarrassed at times – but I cannot say it any other way: her love for us, and ours for her, simply overrode all apparent inadequacies. People would just overlook any awkwardness and enjoy her personality.

One of the favourite things I salvaged from her household after her death was a red Parker pencil. She would always have it lying next to the telephone where she would try to note down – usually with little success – telephone numbers of people who had called. I use the pencil daily and it repeatedly reminds of the irony of fate. During her lonely years on the farm, being able to read surely would have made life a little more bearable. But it also reminds me of how far she came with so few resources.

After decades of having known only bits and pieces of this historical family background, it is only now –twenty-three years after the death of my mother – that I have found a new ethnic home with the Enssle family. In my preschool days we visited family members like Mariechen, but never kept up a constant contact. Then after we passed as white, we did not dare to remain in contact. Also, I had left the country for thirteen years during our time in the States. So I am grateful that, with the writing of this manuscript, I am once again in touch with the Enssles. Needless to say, it has been quite a treat. They get together for family celebrations and special occasions, all belonging to an extensive social network. The parents and grandparents are mostly supported and accepted within the family circle; the younger generation of Enssles have become teachers, doctors and engineers, living in and outside Namibia even as far away as the States. They seem to have become integrated, established individuals in Namibia following the discriminatory laws of apartheid. Compared to my own parents who had cringed at the question "Where are you from?" the young Enssles joke about their Rehoboth background. They laugh about Khoe terms such as /aremiekau – the incomers – the families of mixed background like us who came to live in Rehoboth after the initial historical migration. They tease the older generation about their weird and wonderful traditions of having worn dresses in exemplary condition at the elbows in their adolescent years, lest a suitor should unexpectedly turn up. This is a healthy, modern, relaxed manner of dealing with the past. Everything is out there and open. None of them tried to jump the colour line or pretend to be anybody else other than themselves. They give me the impression that they rode the waves of discrimination, German and South African, stuck it out and emerged healthy on the other side.

Because of the path their lives have taken, the Enssles did not suffer from their mixed background as, for instance, my sister did. Objectively and as a whole, though, our background is no less worthy than that of the next person. Half of our genetic makeup is central European. It was German men who at the turn of the previous century migrated to southern Africa and very quickly became Africanised. While these origins have determined some of our physical appearance, the other half of our genetic makeup is African.

The fact that we were born in Rehoboth and then lived in the area for some years, is neither here nor there. It could equally have been Timbuktu or Grootfontein or Paris. I sense that our Africanness is not bound to a specific locale. It consists of genetic elements of Khoe, a people who have evolved on the continent tens of thousands of years ago and who, some scientists believe, are direct descendants of Man, the species of *Homo,* at the cradle of humanity. They remained behind while some of their Pleistocene cousins migrated across the world, descendants of whom returned to Africa as colonisers, tens of thousands of years later. This, to me, is the romantic but also scientifically exciting aspect of having Khoe genes. After all, it is only a miniscule genetic difference that separates us humans from the chimpanzees. It is the mutation of one gene, "the HERC2, that results in blue eyes; changes to MCIR that causes red hair to sprout instead of black".[132] Is this not a more rewarding approach for southern Africans of mixed heritage to adopt than to follow the one that preaches inadequacies, inferiorities and leads to paralysis in its bearers?

7 WHERE ARE WE ALL FROM? "HUMANITY IS COLOURED"[133]

Since my parents were not of any help to my sister and me in coming to terms with our mixed background, we were forced to seek an explanation for it by ourselves. It was a huge task to make sense of and then to learn to oppose the dominant social thought of the day, namely that being anything but white was inferior, second-rate, even shameful. What I learned, and what I share here, is how historical encounters created communities of mixed background. The same applies to political factors putting us into an apparent demise as a family. In this final chapter, I retrace my steps in trying to find answers to the biological and genetic factors that defined us. Now I realise how exciting this search actually was. For those who wish to delve into its fascinating detail, I invite you to read the relevant endnotes to this chapter.

As a teenager in high school in Cape Town living a white life, I was painfully aware of my mixed background. Once I had realised the obvious reality, I had to hide my heritage. At university, in contrast to the other carefree, confident young adults, I started spending a lot of time and psychological energy grappling with the questions of " Where am I from?" and "Who am I really?" This led me to wonder whether the diffused unease I felt was a result of my supposed lack of wider education, coming from a home devoid of much intellectual stimulation. Or was it the tail end of the habit of hiding? My friends seemed to have a good time, but I was pondering life. At the time I was not even verbalising my issues in terms of identity. I simply longed to be relaxed with myself. It was a nagging, uncomfortable sensation to feel ill at ease with my own being.

People find answers to life's questions in different places. Some in religion. They rest assured that everything around them was created by their concept of an all-powerful being. Others in love. They feel fulfilled and need not look further. Still others, like me, let science instruct their lives.

Once at university, I was drawn to social anthropology. I felt confirmation in its principle of cultural relativity: no single culture is better than any other, they are just different. At least now I could relax about that; we were not culturally inferior to anyone else, at least not according to academics. Now I felt I needed to satisfy my curiosity about "colour". What does it actually mean? How does it come about? This is when biology and genetics became my path. It seems a far cry from the sunburnt pre-schooler on the arid farm in rural Namibia to be explaining her life within the realm of genetics and archaeology, but this ultimately made the most sense to me. In fact, my understanding is that it is everyone's path, primarily because it is the one that connects humanity rather than divides it.

While searching, even before I had come out of the racial closet, I would start to feel drawn to tell aspects of my childhood, all the time carefully editing my stories. For anyone with the patience to listen, I would describe how ou Lenas remained a wonderful example to me, and how I had adopted many values of hers in my own life. People would ask me to describe her. In physical terms, I would remember the striking whiteness of her teeth and the number of prominent moles on her face - and that she had long fingers with pointed fingernails. And then there were those wonderful personal characteristics of hers. She had a strong personality; she was loving. She had an unbeatable sense of humour; she was confident. To me she seemed fearless. I remembered that there were no half measures about her. And yet - in spite of myself - before all of these qualities, I would first recall her extreme blackness. I had to admit that her exceptional skin colour was simply impossible to ignore. In fact, it was difficult to take good photographs of her, because no light reflected off her face.

In contrast to ou Lenas, my father was extraordinarily light-skinned. He had the kind of pigmentation that one would associate with Scandinavian people: a light, sun-sensitive complexion with fine blonde, straight hair and blue eyes. In fact, I learned that he was known as "white Hermann" in Rehoboth.[134] His paleness was as hard to ignore as ou Lenas's blackness. While the difference in appearance between ou Lenas and my father was striking, it wasn't too unusual in the wider Rehoboth area, where the physical appearances of people ranged widely. Even beyond Rehoboth, it is a simple fact of life that some people have flatter noses than others, that some have brown eyes and others green eyes.

Scientifically, what is the source of the difference between ou Lenas and my father? Pigmentation? I wondered what exactly pigmentation is. How deep does it go? To find the answer, I needed to turn to biology. Biology and its sub-discipline, genetics, is complex and can lead to discrimination and misuse. However, it can no longer be ignored when discussing the issue of colour. Genetics tells us that cells, the smallest functional unit of biological life, in the lower layers of the skin of a dark-skinned person will produce more colour than will the cells of a person with a lighter complexion. I found it reassuring that the most obvious aspect of people of colour, namely the shade of their skin, was such a minor distinction.[135]

But biology goes further. It taught me that all humans everywhere in the world have the exact same set of genes. Our genes are the code that defines us as human - as compared to dolphin or donkey - that makes it possible for us to reproduce as a species. Our genes and DNA are found inside virtually each cell of our bodies as building blocks. They are like codes that determine the colour of our skin, as in the case of ou Lenas, the shape of our eyes and how much hair is on our heads. "They generate the shape of our skull, the features of our faces, and the overall contours of our bodies. They influence our likelihood of getting particular diseases. They are the biological foundation on which we build our lives."[136] And where does the encoded information come from? From our parents and their parents and their parents, on and on ... going back many generations. All this information is stored in our genes.[137]

I became increasingly interested. When we look around us, we see undeniable physical differences between people. If I look at our two sons, it is obvious that one of them has a shape of nose resembling my husband's, whereas the other has a shape of nose that more closely resembles mine. These differences are found in each family. Biologists tell us that this is related to the way our genetic material combines. "Many of the genes come in slightly different versions. These differences in the DNA sequences of our genes lie at the basis of our physical uniqueness."[138] Any physical trait that distinguishes one person from another is a handful of combinations within three billion nucleotides within ten trillion cells in our bodies, which are the same in all of us, irrespective of colour. This was yet another biological fact that eased my anxiety about my heritage.[139]

For a long time, people have tried to use the physical differences between groups to divide human beings into distinct categories or "races".[140] Many schemes have been proposed, but none of them have worked. If we look around us, we will see that "humans just don't sort into neat biological categories, despite all the attempts of human societies to create and enforce such distinctions ... In fact, all people are closely related to innumerable lines of descent that defeat any attempt to divide humans into races."[141] These miniscule differences in the DNA sequences of our genes lie at the base of our physical uniqueness. We are basically all the same, yet minimally different. [142]

The physical differences within a group are usually much greater than those between groups, contrary to what racists believe. This is what Eugen Fischer discovered. Doing research among the Rehobothers in 1908, he carefully calibrated shape of eyelids, the shape of the ears. He noted the almond shape of people's eyes and measured earlobes, investigated the texture of hair and the flaring of nostrils. He finally published his findings in a voluminous work.[143] On the basis of his conclusions and deductions, he recommended to the German colonial government that additional mixed marriages should be prohibited. He then returned to his native Baden Württemberg in Germany, where to his surprise, he found exactly the same variety of physical features in the local residents, which in Rehoboth he had attributed to racial factors.[144]

It was extremely satisfying for me to learn that I share the vast majority of genetic material with the rest of the human population. "The genetic variants affecting skin colour and facial features probably involve a few hundred of the billions of nucleotides in a person's DNA – an insignificant amount."[145] Yet, based on these miniscule biological differences, regimes have been built. Millions of people were enslaved because of their skin colour, combined with the religious perception that these people had no souls. And Hitler erroneously spoke of the "Jewish race", while there were only cultural differences of religion, and at most, language. German Jews were German. There must be another reason, another modus operandi to explain why one group of people chooses to emphasise physical differences in another group. It does not require any research to come to the conclusion that the reason is largely economic, with profit as the bottom line.

Having learned the workings of basic genetics and how miniscule are the differences between people of varying colours, I was released from the shame and guilt I had felt for not being "pure" white. Examining where we all came from, namely the origin of mankind, not only helped me to feel at one with humanity, but actually made me proud of my origins. This was all very exciting![146] Suffice it to say here that "according to our DNA, every person alive is descended from a relatively small group of Africans who lived between 100,000 and 200,000 years ago. At that point, perhaps 20,000 people constituted the population from whom we are all descended."[147] The point is that this small group of modern Africans went forth and populated the rest of the world. Their children begot children and those children again bred further children, all the while passing on their genes in the manner we described above. "No matter what the complexities, the genetic evidence available today points to a straightforward conclusion"[148], namely that we are all related.

But humans beings have been on the move ever since their first migrations into Eurasia seventy thousand years ago, either by choice or by force. As an example very much later, through forced removal alone, ten million African slaves were taken to central and southern America before 1870. An estimated five million came to Europe in this manner. Their genes intermixed with those of the local population, all the while carrying the genetic information from generations before them. Slaves were also brought to the Cape of Good Hope, as I've described. In short, my genetic past is no different from that of most of us. We are all mixed, and "contemporary science is now confirming: we are all the bearers of the same mixed genetic *bredie* [stew]. Humanity is Coloured."[149]

On the occasion of the adoption of the new constitution of South Africa in 1996, Thabo Mbeki delivered a famous and moving speech which begins: "I am an African".[150] In essence, he could have been talking for all of us when he said:

The ordination of Jakobus Beukes (centre) as pastor in Rehoboth in 1953, with Pastor Lind (r.) and Preses Diehl (l.). ELCRN Archive

I owe my being to the Khoi and the San whose desolate souls haunt the great expanses of the beautiful Cape – they who fell victim to the most merciless genocide our native land has ever seen ... I am formed by the migrants who left Europe to find a new home on our native land. Whatever their own actions, they remain still a part of me. In my veins courses the blood of Malay slaves who came from the East. Their proud dignity informs my being, their culture is part of my essence ... I am the grandchild of the warrior men and women that Hintsa and Sekhukhune led, the patriots that Cetshwayo and Mephu took to battle, the soldiers Moshoeshoe and Ngungunyane taught never to dishonour the cause of freedom ... I am the grandchild that lays fresh flowers on the Boer graves at St. Helena and the Bahamas ... I come of those who were transported from India and China, those being resided in the fact, solely, that they were able to provide physical labour, who taught me that we could both be at home and be foreign ...

As for Mbeki, so it is for the majority of us. He relates his ethnicity, his Africanness, to a process over time, a diversity of heritage reaching back in history. It is virtually impossible to randomly categorise people. In a small way, I am living evidence of that.

As mentioned earlier, I discovered in 2015 that my parents had been initially classified white. On the occasion of their marriage in 1944, the certificate proclaimed they were coloured, but they were reclassified back to their initial category of white in 1963. I was wondering how much more random it could get. My initial response was complete confusion. I was thinking back to the time my parents had travelled across countries, trying to have my sister born far away from coloured Rehoboth, while they had sent me a thousand

"Original marriage certificate" for Herman Dentlinger and Willemina Ensele (sic), 25 January 1944, signed by Pastor Lind. Reclassifications in 1962 and 1963 by Pastor Jakobus Beukes

kilometres away from the farm to be educated under white conditions. Was this reclassification the consequence of these undertakings, or had it all been unwarranted? Had all the separation and heartache been unnecessary? Did we actually *not* jump the colour line? Was my psychological wrestling with my questions of identity all in vain? Then my confusion turned to anger. Just as with Hedi, the powers-that-be had been playing with our lives! Did they realise the consequences these classifications can have on people's lives? How dare they! But thank goodness, in the end – just as for Hedi before her trial – logic prevailed.

Perhaps in the 1940s and 1950s pastors were instructed to establish the racial categories of their flock. Presumably they used occasions like deaths, births, and marriages to get the classifications up to date. If couples married in Rehoboth or the wider area, were they automatically classified coloured? The argument could have been that if they were white, they would have gone to Namibia's capital, Windhoek.[151] Did my parents know about the contradiction in their classification? I will never know the answer. What I do know is that the law of the land was inconsistent in applying its racial classifications. During the 1950s, racial classification was community-orientated: where you lived, where you were accepted, determined who you were. It was this situation Hedi was hoping to use as an opportunity to move to Swakopmund. It worked for her up to a point. During her trial in Karibib, though, it was phenotype, the physical appearance, that was used as a criterion for classification. In 1951 the first census under the apartheid regime was held. By the mid-1960s, racial classification was based on the recorded responses to "the census form [of 1951], birth registrations and documents that people used to apply for identity documents. In short, criteria were shifted from those of 'community acceptance' in the early 50s to a purely administrative and bureaucratic matter of descent derived from paperwork during the late 1960s."[152] The reason for this lack of interest in actual genetic indicators was that many white families were descended from black ancestors.

I can no longer remember exactly when I received my first identity document, but it was probably during the mid-1960s. Certainly I do not remember ever possessing an identity card or document that had C for "Coloured" stamped on it in bright red ink.[153] Luckily I did not fall into the category of approximately a hundred thousand borderline cases of people whose racial category was doubtful and who had to go through the excruciating experience of having it established.[154] To all intents and purposes, my classification never appeared to be in doubt – at least not from the outside.

The very regime that created the idea of the Verwoerdian[155] categories of White, Coloured, Asian and Black was unable to consistently implement its plan. Its obvious failure to force people into distinct racial categories proves that this is not possible, in spite of changing the parameters. The government could not consistently decide which category we belonged to. Consequently, we jumped between the colour lines.

In my experience, "racial" classifications are random and arbitrary, illogical and useless. Genetically I know where I stand.[156] My deep ancestry shows that, in fact, I am no different to a vast majority of people living in Europe and Asia today. I am just like everybody else.

I am grateful to my ancestors for my genetic makeup. I like it. I have grown fond of my brown, by now greying, somewhat curly hair, probably a mutation from one of my Khoe ancestors. I like my stature, rather tall for a female. This might be a genetic trait from my Germanic forefathers. I would not like to exchange these for any others. Genetics aside, I choose where I want to be, who I want to be. I have chosen to move between different cultures, languages and geographical areas. I know that the behaviour I portray is learned and can be unlearned again. I love speaking French (albeit broken) in France, Afrikaans in South Africa, and the remnants of Khoe taught to me by ou Lenas – and which I later studied at the University of Cape Town – when I am in the rural areas of Namibia. Speaking these different languages has nothing to do with my genetic background. Anybody can learn any language. When I move in the wide-open, arid spaces of southern Africa, I feel a pronounced sense of wellbeing. I know this comes from my heritage and I cherish it. I laugh easily. I sense that this is reminiscent of people like my mother and ou Lenas, who had similarly drifted towards the lightness of life, in spite of its burdens. When I feel the sun on my body, the breeze in my hair, it awakens images in my soul that I cannot always put into words. I feel all of that. I know that it reaches back to a world often intangible and inaccessible, but it is there, a mixture of images, fleeting glimpses and indescribable sensations. I feel all of that and am at ease.

EPILOGUE

It seems like an eternity ago that I first walked into Basel Afrika Bibliographien in 1997 and started telling Dag Henrichsen about Hedi's experiences. Being from Namibia himself, he of course knew and understood. Now, almost two decades and many versions of the story later, three people mentioned in my narratives have since passed away. My sister died in 2001 ten years after the death of our mother; in 2011 my father died, and he was followed by Ou Lenas in 2012. Hedi has always maintained: "I still want to read it before I die" and so she will. I once complained to the historian Ciraj Rassool, how slowly things were progressing. Always ready with a fitting answer, he said something to the effect of: "A project like this is a life's journey." How right he was. During these years I have travelled to many places both real and psychological, that I would not have done had I not had my personal destination in mind. Some of these places I have shared here in my book.

I am content knowing that Hedi will see the seminal story of her life in print. I hope others, too, will read my narratives. Friends and neighbours living outside South Africa or Namibia are amazed and curious when I present an extract from the manuscript or relate an odd detail of my childhood in rural Namibia. They cannot believe that someone in their midst had relatives exposed to discrimination in the way members of my family were. This tells me that even today, although educated, some middle-aged Europeans need to have their memories refreshed regarding apartheid conditions. I quickly grasp the opportunity to compare our predicament to that of the more than one million refugees to Germany alone. Will there be a political right-wing backlash? I ask my small group of listeners or readers to consider how they will act should this come about. Will they oppose a political system that unreasonably discriminates against others?

Particularly, though, I hope to have touched the hearts and consciences of those southern Africans who still shy away from admitting their mixed heritage. Sadly, this includes members of my own family. There is no more reason to pretend to be someone we are not. Both the South African and Namibian constitutions today have as their cornerstone the equality of the individual before the law, irrespective of race, colour or ethnic origin. We need no longer hide or run from the law. We can admit our mixed ethnic origins. In fact, it is far healthier, more interesting and becomes personally more satisfying to step outside the protective *laager* we might have built around us.

It is worthwhile to do so, even if only for the sake of our children. Determined not to have the same happen to them as did to us, I took my boys from a very early age onwards to visit different ethnic environments. I enticed them to visit Warm Springs Reservation in Oregon. We took trips into

With Martha Fischer (right) and my sons Robert and Stephan at Sout Rivier on the Kuiseb River, 2000

the Namib Desert to look up former informants turned friends. Now young men, my sons agree with me that this exposure at a young age made them familiar with people of different colours and cultures. Beyond this I am relieved to know that urban youngsters in South Africa hardly see colour. In the end, it is exposure that breaks down barriers.

And as for me? I am certainly relieved to no longer have to answer the question: "When are you finishing with your book?" Writing about my journey has brought closure to years of doubt, fear, apprehension and anxiety. I sense that I am at the threshold of a new phase in my life. I feel confident to be more outspoken about matters of ethnic background. I feel that now I step into the wider world more seasoned, with a deeper understanding of how social processes can impinge on people's lives unasked, and how individuals and families, particularly children, are forced to deal with these. This insight should not go to waste. I will speak up against discrimination wherever I can.

ACKNOWLEDGEMENTS

Many people have become companions on this journey of mine. I cannot possibly mention each individually, but would like to extend a collective thank you to them all.

For much of the way, my immediate family was forced to come along on this search for the meaning of my background. Over the years, Robert has kept my interest in evolution and particularly genetics alive. Stephan, having of late developed a pronounced interest in literature and language, has often helped to find a fitting phrase and appropriate argument, particularly during the final phases of writing. My husband, Hans, remained mostly in the background, while providing the base from which I could pursue my interest.

Basler Afrika Bibliographien, and Dag Henrichsen in particular, have made it possible for me to realise a long-time dream of telling where I am from. Dag, inherently interested in anything historical and Namibian, has been a patient, calm force over the years as my narrative developed. I thank him for this.

Through Basler Afrika Bibliographien and their many rich educational and research contacts, I made the acquaintance of Ruth Coetzee. As an editor, Ruth has been a pleasure to work with. In a collegial manner she expertly and magically was able to transform raw ideas into a literal pleasure. I have learned a lot from her.

My friend and fellow writer, Sue du Mesnil, did not tire of reading incomplete versions of difficult chapters, discussing fragments of thoughts and then shaping them into a coherent final product.

I cannot do without mentioning Marie Smit, our Afrikaans teacher from the German school, where she taught for forty years. She has been a shining example to her former students, of how learning can be a positive experience. My knowledge of present Afrikaans I owe largely to her. She, too, has read early chapters. Recently she accompanied me to Riebeeck Kasteel, where we located the house my parents briefly lived in during 1959. Even at the age of eighty-three, she remains a constant source of enthusiasm, support and interest.

My thanks go to the staff of the National Archives of Namibia for their support when I arrived unannounced and with little time, searching for relevant material. Particularly Werner Hillebrecht has shown interest in this project while I was writing.

Willie Haacke, former professor of African Languages at University of Namibia took time to check my Khoekhoegowab terms. I thank him for his time and effort and hope we will have more dinners together in Windhoek.

I share my interest in Rehoboth with my friend and historian, Cornelia Limpricht. Being an accepted authority on Rehoboth, she willingly answered my many (repeated) questions on Rehoboth details from wherever she was at the time.

Last but not least, I thank all of my relatives, not only in Windhoek but also in Rehoboth, for having opened their doors to me. I appreciate the new home I found with them. I thank the Benades, particularly Liesbeth, for their warmth and hospitality, and Lien for showing me other sides of Rehoboth. I am deeply grateful for the meaningful times we could spend together after all these years.

ENDNOTES

1   Namibia had been mandated to South Africa since 1921 – a League of Nations decision following the loss of its protectorate Deutsch Südwest Afrika by the Germans post-World War I. As such, the country progressively had apartheid laws imposed upon it.

2   I would like to thank historian, Ciraj Rassool, for this expression. I hope he reads this one day.

3   Sandelowsky maintains it takes up to ten years of regular rainfall and proper management for pasture to recover from a state of total overgrazing. [Sandelowsky, B. Archaeologically Yours (Namibia Scientific Society, Windhoek, 2004) p. 61.]

4   *Calafractus alexandri.*

5   German thorn tree (common name) or *Prosopis africana*.

6   Pearson, P. "The History and Social Structure of the Rehoboth Baster Community of Namibia", MA thesis, University of Witwatersrand, Johannesburg,1986, p. 13.

7   ibid.

8   Limpricht, C. "Churches of Rehoboth" in Limpricht, C. (ed.) Rehoboth, Namibia: Past and Present (Solitaire Press, Windhoek, 2012) p. 262.

9   Sandelowsky, B. Archaeologically Yours p. 59ff.

10 ibid. p.192. This monument was in the shape of a mini-amphitheatre.

11 Limpricht, C. in Rehoboth, Namibia p. 110ff.

12 This figure is given by the latest census of 2012 of Rehoboth whereas residents on farms in the Gebiet could be in excess of 3,000 [personal communication, Cornelia Limpricht.]

13 Limpricht, C. in Rehoboth, Namibia p. 263. See also Pearson, P. "The History" p. 13.

14 "It required a combined force of police, troops and three aircraft by the South Africans to quell the Rehoboth rebellion". [Carstens, P. Opting out of Colonial Rule: The Brown Voortrekkers of South Africa and their Constitutions (Witwatersrand University Press, 1984) p. 27. See also Britz, R., Limpricht, C. & Lang, H. A Concise History of the Rehoboth Baster (Hess Publishers, Windhoek, 1999) p. 33.]

15 In 1990 the term Khoekhoegowab replaced that of Nama for the language spoken by Namibian Khoe and Dama people.

16 Britz, R. et al. A Concise History p. 11.

17 Elphick, R. and Malherbe, V. "The Khoisan to 1828" in The Shaping of South African Society, 1652-1840 Elphick, R. and Giliomee, H. (eds.) (Maskew Miller Longman, Cape Town,1989) p. 110.

18 Armstrong, J. and Warden, N. "The Slaves, 1652-1834" in The Shaping of South African Society p. 111.

19   Madagascar contributed 48.5% of company slaves for the Cape, with India and Indonesia each contributing 15.8%, with 19.8% being from other origins. [Armstrong, J. and Warden, N. in The Shaping of South African Society p. 121.]

20   ibid. p. 109.

21   ibid. p. 124.

22   Elphick, R and Shell, R. "Intergroup relations: Khoikhoi, settlers, slaves and free blacks, 1652-1795" in The Shaping of South African Society p. 195.

23   ibid. p. 196.

24   ibid. p. 195.

25   For instance, as was often the custom, van der Boogaerden, the commander of the return fleet, sold his female slave Catharina of Bengal at the Cape. It appears a second transaction took place when Jan Woutersz van Middelburg paid for her freedom. Only then could he marry her, since marriage with a slave in bondage (and non-Christian) was frowned upon. The couple went to live on Robben Island, where Woutersz van Middelburg was the overseer and where their first child was born. It is possible they were sent to this isolated island because of the controversy such unions produced in the Cape society. [Heese, H. Groep sonder Grense: Die rol en status van die gemengde bevolking aan die Kaap, 1652-1795 (Protea Boekhuis, Pretoria, 2005) p. 23, quoting Böeseken: "Slaves and free Blacks at the Cape, 1658-1700" p. 78.]

26   Guelke, L. "Freehold farmers and frontier settler, 1657-1780" in The Shaping of South African Society p. 70.

27   ibid. p. 73.

28   ibid. p. 74.

29   From 1743 onwards, burghers could apply for permits to loan farms and convert parts of these into freehold tenure on payment of a lump sum based on the value of the property.

30   In 1751 Rudolph Brits registered the loan farm Schoenmakersfontein.[Penn, N. "The Orange Frontier Zone, c.1700-1805" in Smith, A. (ed.) Einiqualand Studies of the Orange River Frontier (UCT Press, Cape Town, 1995) p. 31.]

31   Heese, H. Groep sonder Grense p. 45.

32   An exception to this is the early marriage of Eva, as she was called after her baptism, to the official, Pieter van Meerhoff on 2 June, 1664. [Schoeman, K. Seven Khoi Lives; Cape Biographies of the seventeenth century (Protea Book Press, Pretoria, 2009) p. 27.]

33   Further to the note above, it is recorded that Eva, the Khoekhoe employee of Van Riebeeck's household, married Pieter van Meerhoff at

the Cape. Elphick, R. and Shell, R. in The Shaping of South African Society p. 194.

34 ibid. p. 198.

35 There were 420 male slaves compared to 100 female slaves in 1711. Heese, H. in Groep sonder Grense p. 44.

36 Arnoldus Willemsz Basson of Wessel, a wealthy farmer.

37 Elphick, R. and Shell, R. in The Shaping of South African Society p. 198.

38 ibid. p. 201.

39 Penn, N. Rogues, Rebels and Runaways Eighteenth-Century Cape Characters (David Philip Publishers, Cape Town, 1999) p. 92.

40 Du Preez, M. The Pale Native: Memories of a Renegate Reporter (Zebra Press, Cape Town, 2004) p. 25ff.

41 In 1775 it was decreed in Stellenbosch that individuals of this description "should be bound to serve their masters until the age of 25", thus spending nearly half their lifetimes in unpaid labour. [Penn, N. Rogues, Rebels and Runaways p. 95.]

42 Guelke, L. in The Shaping of South African Society p. 82.

43 Penn, N. Rogues, Rebels and Runaways p. 166.

44 Escaping was not without its dangers. These illegal refugees were dealt with severely. Initially, runaway slaves were most brutally maimed when recaptured to deter them from leaving their rightful masters. They were capital for their owners, to dispose of as their masters wished. We have read the gruesome treatment they were subject to. According to the order of the day in 1711 at the Cape, a first offender would not only be whipped but also be branded on the cheek. Caught after a second escape, a man would be branded on the other cheek. If unlucky enough to be caught a third time, he would have his nose and ears cut off. This did not necessarily deter slaves from attempting escape. It was their only form of protest against a system that was so violent, that Penn rhetorically remarks: "It is, perhaps, unnecessary to explain why a slave should wish to run away from a regime where such punishments were permissible". [Penn, N. Rogues, Rebels and Runaways p. 74.]

45 Coetzee, J.M. Dusklands (Vintage Books, New York, 2004) p. 109.

46 Penn, N. in Einiqualand Studies p. 23.

47 These had revolted in 1733 and again in 1739, the latter revolt having been brutally crushed by farmers as recruits in the commando system.

48 The most famous of these groups were the Afrikaners under their leader, Jonker Afrikaner. They crossed the Orange River in the 1820s and then continued to spread havoc in southern Namibia until Jonker's death in 1861. For 38 years he came to dominate the trade and resources of southern and central Namibia. The other group famous in Namibia was that of the Witboois, led by Hendrik Witbooi.

49   Wallace, M. A History of Namibia. From the Beginning to 1990 (Jacana Media, Johannesburg, 2011) p. 59ff.

50   The communities from whom the current Rehobothers stem lived along the middle Orange River at places like Pella, de Tuin, Kenhardt, Steinkopf, Concordia, Loeriesfontein.

51   Limpricht, C. in Rehoboth, Namibia p. 23 ff.

52   They had made repeated attempts, mostly with the help of their resident missionaries at the time, Schröder and Heidmann, to acquire land in the manner it was made available to white stock farmers .

53   Pearson, P. "The History and Social Structure" p. 39 ff.

54   ibid. p. 54.

55   A memorandum, signed by their then missionary Heidmann, their catechist Schroeder, and 169 others, was drawn up in March 1866 for submission to the Governor. Pearson, P. "The History and Social Structure" p. 55.

56   ibid. p. 56.

57   The raiders were called Koranna, themselves a heterogeneous Khoe-speaking loosely organised community formerly having lived a mobile lifestyle, but having lost their lands to encroaching Boers.

58   On 24 February a historical meeting by 40 heads of 58 families is recorded as having been held at de Tuin.

59   The latest account tells how the group was led by Hermanus van Wyk accompanied by the Rhenish missionary, Friedrich Heidmann and his wife Ida, and how they finally settled at Rehoboth in 1845 having agreed to purchase - albeit controversially - the land from Abraham Swartbooi, head of the Swartbooi Khoe group. There the community has remained until this day. [Limpricht, C. and Lang, H. "The Trek of the Rehoboth Basters in Rehoboth" in Rehoboth, Namibia p. 8.]

60   Nimako, K. and Willemsen, G. The Dutch Atlantic: Slavery, Abolition and Emancipation (Pluto Press, London, 2011) pp. 16 and 25.

61   ibid. p.158.

62   An expression used by Zoe Wicomb in David's Story (Kwela Books, Cape Town, 2002) p. 34.

63   Limpricht, C. and Lang, H. "The Trek" in Rehoboth, Namibia p. 26.

64   Limpricht, C. "Families, and Farms, Mixed Marriages in Rehoboth during German Colonial Times in Rehoboth" in Rehoboth, Namibia p. 147.

65   There is obviously a discrepancy between the dates given. I tend towards accepting Hedi's date. It is supported by officer von Burgsdorff, who on March 1897 finds four former German soldiers married to Grootfontein women, one of them being Dentlinger. See relevant endnote in Ch. 6.

66   This is my term distinguishing between the architecture of homes built in a linear fashion, one room attached to the next with individual entrances all from the verandah, and those, such as the Kwartel house where the design has interlinking rooms.

67   A term used by Gabriel Fagan in Brakdak. Flatroofs in the Karoo (Breestraat Publikasies, Cape Town, 2008).

68   Democratic Turnhalle Alliance, a leading political party prior to Namibian independence

69   These refer to the South African currency, also used in Namibia until 1961.

70   When I listened to this, I was sceptical. Then I found a reference to this in Carstens, P. "Always Here Even Tomorrow: The Enduring Spirit of the Southern African Nama" in The Modern World (Xlibris, USA, 2007) p. 166.

71   To anybody living in Namibia it would immediately have been evident that genetically she was a Dama or Damara person. Even though they were talented metalworkers, historically the Dama people were looked down upon by other pastoralists such as the Nama and particularly the Herero, and were in fact made servants by these people. They were called "gou-Dama" (shit-Dama) by the Herero. In the Gebiet, it is the Nama and Damara who occupy the lowest level in the racial hierarchy.

72   At the start of World War I, South Africa, its neighbour to the south, siding against Germany had invaded the then German protectorate of Südwest Afrika, and conquered it by 1915. It subsequently quickly established its rule on the territory. Having lost the war, Germany relinquished all its colonies, including its protectorate of present day Namibia. A decision in 1920 by the then League of Nations gave South Africa mandateship of the country. Once the status of martial law was lifted on 1 January 1921, South Africa incrementally began to establish a political and administrative structure. Thereafter, the passing of several proclamations in parliament in South Africa shaped the legal climate to its own liking and advantage. The most incisive of these was the Native Administration Proclamation no. 11/1922 (SWA) which initiated the establishment of reserves. Increasingly, the policy of separate development took shape, classifying the population into ethnic groups. Increasingly also, the power to implement the laws of "native affairs" was shifted away from the administrator, the de facto head of the administration in the country, to the South African parliament. [Tötemeyer, G. South West Africa/ Namibia: Facts, Attitudes, Assessments and Prospects (Focus Suid Publishers, Randburg, 1977) p. 13.]

73 Even though this is how the apartheid regime phrased the distinctions between citizens, the differences were not strictly speaking "racial". People with the kind of genetic mix we had, were not a different race. We might have belonged to a different ethnic group, meaning we had a slightly different genetic and slightly different cultural mix than the average urban white, but we continued to share by far the same genetic and cultural set of indicators with the rest of the citizens of the land. I therefore use the word "race" strictly to relate to genetic elements. It has become a concept too confused with cultural differences. I believe it should actually be disused.

74 National Archives of Namibia: LKA/1/3/12;6.1.55 Art.1 Prok. No.19 van 1934 soos gewysig deur Ord. 20/1953 en Ord.13/1954 en Art.2 van Ord. No.19/1934.

75 According to the South West African Constitution Act 42 of 1925, only whites had the franchise. Tötemeyer, G. South West Africa/ Namibia p. 12.

76 He did this by dubious means, exploiting the inexperience and trust of local leaders, some of whom "had little or no control over the land they claimed to sell". [Wallace, M. A History p. 117.]

77 The first of these purchases occurred on 1 May 1883. It comprised the bay of Angra Pequena, now Lüderitz Bay, with adjoining land of five-mile radius in all directions for the sum of £100 and 200 guns. [Schoedder, E., Otto, A. and Rusch, W. "Lüderitzbucht damals und gestern" in Namibia Wissenschaftliche Gesellschaft (1987) p. 3.]

78 However, I have found no evidence to corroborate this version of Hedi's story, neither in the National Archives in Windhoek nor in the Cape Town archives. In the real sense of the word, however, we are living proof of some such version of it being true, as are some scanty literary references of later dates.

79 Soldiers at times left the Schutztruppe quite soon after having arrived in Südwest Afrika [personal communication, Cornelia Limpricht.]

80 Apparently he ran his establishment in a manner fashioned according to his Swabian origin complete with a bowling alley. [Rövenkamp, W. Südwest - nach einem Tagebuch über Erlebnisse in Deutsch-Südwestafrika Anfang des zwanzigsten Jahrhunderts (Books on Demand GmbH, Norderstedt, Germany, 2010) p. 185ff.]

81 "'Colour' is ... used as a label for a kind of compendium of features that are subsequently racially typical ... A dark skin colour; dark eyes, with a mongolian lid; a broad, flat nose; and dark, frizzy (kroes) hair, are undesirable features associated with Khoi or other 'non-white' ancestry. Desirable features are a light skin, a narrow nose, light-coloured eyes,

and straight, light-coloured hair." [Pearson, P. "The History and Social Structure" p. 500.]

82 Hans Beukes presents a more extended version of this incident. [Beukes, H. Long Road to Liberation (Porcupine Press, Johannesburg, 2014) p. 23.]

83 Wicomb, Z. Playing in the Light (The New Press, New York, 2006) p. 123.

84 Here her revised version of the story becomes somewhat confusing. Surely it would have been clear to the immigration officials that German was spoken in Namibia's mandate? However, this is how she told it.

85 During my research in the Namib Desert and in the Richtersveld I learned how Khoe stock-owners would jointly own herds of goats and sheep, one relative being responsible for the care of the animals. This was not too different from the system of cooperation my relatives applied.

86 Sandelowsky, B. Archaeologically Yours pp. 38-39.

87 Pearson, P. "The History and Social Structure" p. 499ff.

88 Wallace, M. A History of Namibia p. 214. Corporal punishment (mostly meaning flogging) had been introduced by the Germans in 1907, a väterliches Züchtigungsrecht as part of the Native Ordinances or Eingeborenenverordnungen, [ibid. p. 186.] but had been abolished by the South African administration in 1920.

89 Pearson, P. "The History and Social Structure" p. 25.

90 Limpricht, C. "Biography of Narais Farm, Landownership in Rehoboth" in Rehoboth Namibia p. 394.

91 Fugard, A. Cousins: A Memoir (Witwatersrand University Press, Johannesburg, 1994) p. 33.

92 On rare occasions this kind of flooring will be found in caves. See for instance, Sandelowsky, B. Archaeologically Yours p. 125.

93 Breckenridge, K. "The Book of Life: The South African Population Register and the Invention of Racial Descent, 1950-1980" in Kronos South African Histories 40 (University of Western Cape, Bellville, 2014) p. 232.

94 Namibian friends of a similar age to me have similarly mentioned this total disregard of communication with children about issues that actually concern them. Some tell how parents would send them to schools, enrol them at universities with no discussion of any of these plans with their children. Asking my cousin what she felt about our background, her immediate reply was, "The worst was that our parents told us nothing."

95 Fischer-Buder, I. (ed.) 100 Jahre Deutsche Schule Kapstadt (Creda Press, Cape Town,1983) p. 33ff.

96 In March 2013, I made the trip to Riebeeck Kasteel with Marie Smit –
    Afrikaans and Geography teacher at the German School since 1959 – to
    try to find the house we had lived in during 1958/9. The village has
    changed considerably. With the help of Suzanne Duminy and her hus-
    band, we finally agreed that it could only have been the present mod-
    ern self-catering complex on the corner of Heuwel and Piet Retief
    Street belonging to the Duminys. I thank both Suzanne and her hus-
    band for their time and interest in my project, and for the bag of
    almonds from the trees I played in as a child 53 years ago.

97 Substitution of section 7 of Proclamation 19 of 1934.

98 National Archives: The Laws of SWA:1953, 349.688 SWA, 1953, p. 26.

99 See www.intermix.org.uk/features/FEA_13_zoe_wicomb.

100 Perhaps, Manfred, you will read this one day and accept my apprecia-
    tion 40 years later.

101 Taken from the title of Zoe Wicomb's book.

102 Incidentally, Louisa pointed out the difference between *kleitjie* and
    kross (Rehoboth pronunciation for *kaross*). She maintained that a kleit-
    jie was used as a mat, whereas a kaross was used as a cover, for a bed
    for instance, like a *vel* kombers – a hide blanket. She added that the
    word "kaross" leaned towards the Nama.

103 There was a form of marriage negotiations to be followed on similar
    lines as in the case of Lena. [Pearson, P. "The History and Structure"
    p. 511.]

104 According to Pearson, marriages were arranged mostly in the upper
    classes, whereby we were not aware that we belonged there. [ibid.
    p. 512.]

105 His gravestone in the cemetery in Windhoek erroneously shows a year
    of birth of 1880, when in fact his actual date of birth is 29 July 1879 and
    the date of his death is recorded as 27 February 1940. When mentioned
    in archival documents relating to business deals, his name is sometimes
    spelled "Ensle".

106 Wede married his Rehoboth partner lawfully in church in 1897 and sub-
    sequently went to considerable effort to have the church wedding rec-
    ognised as a civil wedding in the registry in Rehoboth. When this was
    denied, he wrote a complaint about these circumstances to Reichs-
    Chancellor von Bülow. Obviously being concerned about the education
    of his children, he was one of several men who applied to found a school
    in Rehoboth. When this did not materialise he subsequently sent his
    children to be educated in Germany. [Limpricht, C. "Families, and
    Farms" in Rehoboth, Namibia p. 154.]

107 This incident is told in greater detail by Cornelia Limpricht. [ibid. p. 158.]

108 ibid. p. 148.

109 He died on 25 March 1940 in the Catholic Hospital in Windhoek.

110 National Archives: Est. 2581, NAN/NLA.

111 The latter was handed over to the magistrate at Rehoboth under the National Emergency Regulations and was then kept in charge of the Defence Department of Windhoek.

112 She gave a certified declaration that she herself owned 470 goats on the neighbouring farm Korabasin, a farm touching the north-east corner of Gamis, where she paid £1-£10 rent per month.

113 Personal communication, Werner Hildebrecht.

114 However, if Hedi is correct with her date of 1892, it could possibly be that my great-grandfather might even have participated in the attack by von François on Witbooi at Hoornkrans. To briefly recall the historical background, von François was galled by the peace settlement in November 1892 between the two arch-enemies Samuel Maharero and Witbooi, thereby strengthening their indigenous position against the colonisers. [Wallace, M. A History p.128.] Thus, von Francois decided to use the opportunity of the 1893 arrival of reinforcements to punish Witbooi not only for his cooperation with Samuel Maharero, but also really for having consistently refused to bow to German authority. As is well known, he staged a surprise attack on Witbooi at Hoornkrans on 12 April, the outcome of which was Witbooi, women and children all coming to an inhumane and cruel end. [ibid. p. 129.] As yet, I have not found any evidence of whether my great-grandfather actually participated in this attack. It remains supposition on my side.

115 These were the Portuguese Jonnie Annics, the Boer Benade and four former German soldiers of the *Schutztruppe* - Dentlinger, Schmey, Levanezik (Lewanschek) and Kahmann. Von Burgsdorff came across some resistance from these soldiers, who considered their children as German and thus to serve in the *Schutztruppe*, not as "natives".

116 Limpricht, C. "Mixed marriages" in Rehoboth, Namibia p. 147.

117 Cornelia Limpricht (personal communication) tells that it was not unusual for German soldiers to have served only briefly. She states the case of Hagen, who served for only two years from 1894 to 1896. This is confirmed further by both Dr K. Budayk and Werner Hildebrecht of the National Archives, that soldiers would have preferential access to farms and would happily leave the employ of the *Schutztruppe* to become farmers or traders or surveyors or grasp at any other employment opportunity that presented itself.

118 He called his company "G. Dentlinger in Bethanien". He went through the accepted bureaucratic procedures of registration and required announcements in the Deutsches Kolonialblatt: Amtsblatt für die Schutzgebiete des Deutschen Reiches. Jahrgang XV, Berlin, 15 December

1904, Nr.25. On 6 June 1905 he had the name of the company changed to "Gustav Dentlinger in Bethanien", for reasons that remain obscure. Again he went through the required re-registration and announcement procedures in the Deutsches Kolonialblatt on 15 October1905 proper to German - even colonial - bureaucracy.

119 On 4 November 1905.

120 A further letter of 28 April 1906 confirms this.

121 The company retained its name of "Gustav Dentlinger in Bethanien".

122 National Archives: NLA D22, D1.

123 ibid.

124 ibid. His immovable assets included the farm Koankoras, which was not permitted to be included in the insolvency proceedings (possibly because the bond on it was too high) [ibid.] In the auction was included "his plot of 9778 sq. m. registered on his name and situated in the south-east of the place of Bethanie, the residential and business premises and garden surrounded by a stone wall ..." [ibid.] All his personal assets went to the farmer and trader Ferdinand Gessert of the farm Sandverhaar, who had sued him for 13,459.75 Mark.

125 National Archives: NLA 22, D2.

126 The correspondence starting with issues relating to his will signed 1 September 1909 were already written at Rehoboth.

127 Rövenkamp wrote a narrative on the old days of Südwest Afrika (now Namibia) based on the diaries of his grandfather. He admits to having embellished somewhat the life at Bethanie at the time, but if even just the basis is true, then Gustav Dentlinger must have been a man of stature. [Rövenkamp, W. Südwes p.185.]

128 ibid. Röwenkamp admits having freely interpreted the diaries that this story is mentioned in.

129 Henrichsen, D. "... unerwünscht im Schutzgebiet ... nicht schlechthin unsittlich" in Bechhaus-Gerst, M. & Leutner, M. (eds.) Frauen in den deutschen Kolonien M. (Berlin, 2009) pp. 80-90.

130 Quoting the Administrator's Files in the National Archives, Pearson mentions that on 28 November 1928 the Rehoboth Council informed of the resolution requesting compulsory education for all children of the Gebiet. In the case of the Enssles, this probably was difficult to implement because there was no farm school on Gamis. [Pearson, P. "The History and Social Structure".]

131 Recently I found a 1966 letter to my parents, in which I had written: "Mom, you have to read! Next time I write, I will write a page just for you and then you have to try to read it all by yourself, okay?!"

132 Hawks, J. "Evolution, the Human Saga" in Scientific American (special issue, September 2014) p. 89.

133 Cronin, J. "Creole Cape Town" in Watson, S. (ed.) Cape Town: A city Imagined and the Meanings of a Place (Penguin, Johannesburg, 2005) p. 45. I thank Jeremy Cronin for letting me use his quote as a subtitle to my chapter. He offers this phrase as an alternative to Thabo Mbeki's "I am an African", the title of his memorable speech delivered at the adoption of South Africa's new constitution in1996. Cronin expresses hesitation in using the phrase, saying it is open to misinterpretation. I believe it would have been very fitting.

134 Personal communication, Cornelia Limpricht, 2016.

135 Even though Robert Hooke had first discovered the cell in 1665, naming it after the cells inhabited by monks in a monastry, it was Matthias Jakob Schleiden and Theodor Schwann who developed cell theory in 1839. Cell theory declares that all organisms are composed of one or more cells. It states that cells are the fundamental unit of structure and function in all living organisms, that all cells come from pre-existing cells, and that all cells contain the hereditary information necessary for regulating cell functions and for transmitting information to the next generation of cells. Furthermore, a human cell can only be seen by the naked eye under a microscope; thus it is hard to imagine the following: a human body contains more than ten trillion cells. Human cells have different functions. For instance, if we were to put ou Lenas's skin, or that of any other person with a dark complexion, under a microscope, the cells in the top layer of their skin, the epidermis, would be indistinguishable from anybody else's. But in the lower layers of their epidermis, beneath the surface are layers of cells known as melanocytes. Melanocytes are programmed to give skin its colour. Their main function is to produce melanin. Thus, the melanocytes of a dark-skinned person would produce more of the pigment eumelanin. Eumelanin is one of three kinds of melanin that produces black or brown pigmentation mostly to the skin, as compared to other melanin that might produce a reddish hue or the green of the eyes. The melanocytes of a fair-skinned person would produce less. Ou Lenas's melanocytes would produce a lot of the pigment eumelanin, whereas the melanocytes of my father and myself would produce less eumelanin. Beneath the melanocytes, the differences between that of ou Lenas, and for the sake of argument that of my father's, again fade away. "Every other type of cell in their remaining bodies looks no different from the corresponding cells in any other person." [Olson, S. Mapping Human History. Genes, Race, and Our Common Origins (Mariner Books, New York, 2003) p. 14].

136 Olson, S. Mapping Human History p. 17.

137 Skin colour, of course, is an extremely noticeable attribute. Again looking at ou Lenas and my father, as an example, there are subtler differ-

ences. My father was tall and slim, whereas ou Lenas's build was somewhat wider and shorter. My father had an aquiline nose, whereas ou Lenas's was flatter and wider. The moles on her face were noticeable. He had none. To find the origins of these differences, we have to look into the nucleus, the small compartment that exists, besides others elements, inside almost each and every one of the ten trillion human cells. Floating in the nucleus of most such cells, in a warm bath of nutrients and enzymes, are 46 structures called chromosomes. There are 23 pairs of chromosomes in humans, numbered 1 to 22 in order from longest to shortest . The 23rd pair consists of an X chromosome and a Y chromosome in men and two X chromosomes in women. This last pair of chromosomes determines the gender of any individual. One of each pair of chromosomes is descended from a chromosome in the mother's egg cell; the other chromosome in the pair is descended from a chromosome in the father's sperm cell. Most of us know or have seen a depiction of chromosomes. Often they are shown as an image of twisting bands turning on themselves off the page, implying that they go on and on, which they do since they are very long. If the DNA in the 46 chromosomes of one single human cell were stretched out, it would extend from one end of the kitchen table to the other - six feet in all. [Olson, S. Mapping Human History p. 17.] This image is a representation of chromosomes inside a cell, which at a certain time of the cell's life, scrunch up into stubby cigar-shaped objects. If they are then exposed to a chemical called Giemsa stain, bands appear around the chromosomes like stripes on a croquet mallet. [ibid. p. 15.] This now visible, miraculous structure is also referred to as the "double helix". The term "double" refers to the nature of each strand being complementary to the other running in opposite directions. [Venter, J. Life at the Speed of light. From the Double Helix to the Dawn of Digital Life (Penguin Books, New York, 2014) p. 5.] The image of the strand of the double helix has become quite an icon in our media lives, used in advertisements, websites or as any kinds of emblems. It looks like a coil twisting itself away from us. Except for people with rare chromosomal abnormalities, the banding patterns (how chromosomes are connected) are essentially the same for people anywhere in the world. In order then to find out what exactly it is that brings about the differences between people, chromosomes do not help us much. We will have to look inside chromosomes. Each one of the 22 pairs of chromosomes (within almost each one of the ten trillion cells in our body) contains a single strand of deoxyribonucleic fluid, or DNA. The core of the DNA consists of four simple building blocks (or bases) called nucleotides - adenine, thymine, cytosine and guanine, abbreviated A,T,C and G - strung together in a chain. For example, a particular section of DNA on human chromosome 2 consists of the following nucleotides: ATACTGGTGTGCTGAAT. They line up in a particular manner. But that's just 15 nucleotides. The 23 chromosomes in each human sperm cell or egg cell contain about three billion nucleotides altogether. This might amount to 6,000 nucleotides - more than letters in an average sized book. [Olson, S. Mapping Human History p. 17.] This is hard to imagine. However, bear with me: the manner of combination of the nucleotides - A,T,C and G - the position they take in relation to each other - is like a code, like hardware in a pc giving instructions as to, for instance, the production of eumelanin or the shape of the nose, the head, knock-knees or even moles. Let us take human life a little further. In order for the human race to survive, we have to reproduce. We said above that cells have different functions. We learned how the melanocytes would produce melanin. We learned further that cells are the smallest unit of life that can replicate independently. Thus, it is egg and sperm cells that have the specific job, the function, to regulate the reproductive process. We also said above that each cell contains 23 pairs of chromosomes wound up in a helix shape. One chromosome in each pair is descended from a chromosome in the father's sperm cell; the other is descended from a chromosome in the mother's egg. Very simplified, this proceeds as follows: The double helix splits down the middle, each half recombines with a similar half to once again produce a cell containing the full set of 23 pairs, off to start a new organism. The longer version of this process looks as follows: the first step is for the 23 pairs of chromosomes in the egg cell to duplicate themselves, making exact copies of each half of the DNA (duplication). They end up with two copies of the mother's only 23 chromosomes and two copies of the father's only 23 chromosomes. Once this is done they kind of intertwine with each other exchanging parts of their genes (crossover). They end up having exchanged bits of the mother's genetic material with that of the father's, from the same space, meaning, for instance, chromosomes for hair colour interchange or shape of the knees genes. They end up as two of the same combining genetic elements from both parents (synthesis). The next step is for these combined elements from the father and mother to once again divide, ending up with an egg cell with only 23 chromosomes, however, 23 chromosomes that now are a combination of both the father's and the mother's genes. This cell now travels down the fallopian tube of the woman in search for a sperm cell with also only 23 chromosomes with which it now combines into a new cell complete with 46 chromosomes to start the growth of the embryo in the womb. Now once again, the new cell contains required two pairs of 23 chromosomes, one set of 23 from the mother and the other set of 23 from the father. In turn, their children will pass on their combined genes to their offspring - from one generation to the next and the next and the next. In this manner, ou Lenas has inherited her black complexion from her parents, as well as the moles on her face and her squattish build from her father and mother. I, on the other hand, was given my curly hair, probably by my mother's genes, my lanky frame and fair skin colour from my father's genetic pool. What is notable, though, is that my sister inherited my mother's build, smaller and more petite, even though she kept her thin frame of my father. So, while parents have the same number of genes as their offspring, (in fact, the same as anybody else) it is through the swopping and recombining of genetic material by the chromosomes that even within the same family, one offspring may have red hair inherited from one parent, while the other has blonde hair inherited from the other parent. This is a truly impressive mechanism of evolution!

138 Olson, S. Mapping Human History p. 17.

139 As unbelievable as this system is, even it does not always work perfectly. Considering the vast number of connections and switches that are made by the three billion in total nucleotides, once in a while there are glitches in the alignment of the nucleotides - ATCG. Once in every thousand nucleotides, on average, the two sequences would differ. The genetic material could have been attacked by environmental factors, like severe starvation or there is damage to the genetic material, through some sort of injury of the body, or simple cut and paste errors occur. Bits of the genetic material are deleted, some are doubled. In any of these cases the sequence of the nucleotides does not string up together as it should have. Where perhaps an A was supposed to be, now there is a G. Remember there are three billion of these that have to be replicated in the cells to form the new embryo. So that each new form of life is not an exact replica of its parents. There may be unpredicted changes to the nucleotide sequences, which result in unpredicted results. The point, however, is that this, too, is reflected in the genetic coding, as it becomes established as a new diversion from the former sequence. It can be detected and is noted. Once again, let us take Ou Lenas as an example. It is known that people living close to the equator and who are exposed to excessive ultraviolet light more than perhaps those living in the northern hemisphere, over many generations developed a darker skin colour than their northern counterparts. In other words, over several generations and by utter chance it happened that a certain sequence of nucleotides occurred that led to an increasing darkening of the skin. Through time, individuals with a darker complexion became preferred partners. Perhaps they were better

able to combat the bombardment of ultraviolet rays; perhaps consequently they lived longer. They would subsequently pass on their particular genetic sequence to their offspring and slowly a group of people evolved that have a darker skin colour, merely as a protection against the ultraviolet radiation. Scientists call this a mutation. Here then, at last, is the origin of the genetic differences between individuals and following this, between groups. Once in every thousand nucleotides , on average, the two sequences might differ. One person might have an A at one point, whereas the other has a G. Or a few nucleotides might be added, deleted or transposed in one person but not in another.

140   Meanwhile the word "race" has become so burdened with misconceptions, so weighed down by social baggage, that it serves no useful purpose. The sooner it can be eliminated, the better. I prefer to speak of "biological" or "physical" differences, should we have to point out differences in physical appearance of individuals.

141   Olson, S. Mapping Human History p. 34.

142   In the 18th century the Swedish biologist – his name Latinised to Linnaeus – "devised a classification scheme for all of the species in the world, a total of 12,000. He chose the name of homo sapiens for us humans, meaning wise man. But Linnaeus, careful scientist that he was, went further. When he looked at people from around the world, they seemed to fall into distinct categories on the basis of their appearance. He, therefore, proceeded to define five subspecies: afer, or Africans; americanus or Americans; asiaticus or Asiatics; europaeus or Europeans; and monstrosus, a blatantly racist category that basically included all the people he did not like, including some that turned out to be fictitious. For instance, the flatheads, troglodytes, and dwarves he writes about have never been found". [Wells, S. Deep Ancestry: Inside the Genographic Project: National Geographic Society, Washington 2006) p. 17.] Similar categories of human racial subspecies remained popular until even up to 20 or 30 years ago. They might have been slightly modified as Carlton Coon did in the 1960s. He used essentially the same racial categories as Linnaeus did 200 years ago, only slightly modified: Caucasoids replaces Linnaeus's europaeus, Negroids replaces Linnaeus's afer, Mongoloids, a combination of Linaeus's asiaticus and americanus. Coon added two further categories: Capoid (the Khoesan people of southern Africa) and Australoid (the aboriginal people of Australia and New Guinea).

143   Fischer, E. Die Rehobother Bastards und das Bastardierungsproblem beim Menschen: anthropologische und ethnographiesche Studien am Rehobother Bastardvolk in Deutsch-Südwest-Afrika, ausgeführt mit

Unterstützung der Kgl. Preuss verlag von Fischer, G. (Akademie der Wissenschaften, Jena, 1913).

144 Personal communication, Cornelia Limpricht.

145 Olson, S. Mapping Human History p. 69.

146 The current generally established view is that humans evolved in eastern Africa, within some 500 miles of the equator's passage across the continent. This is of particular importance to us as southern Africans because many notable prehistoric finds have also been made in areas that we actually know well, such as De Kelders on the west coast of South Africa, Kathu Pan 1, or Pinnacle Point on the southern coast of South Africa, or the Erongo or the Namib Desert in Namibia. The fossils recovered by paleoanthropologists - in brief - have told us the following: Around two million years ago, a species of large hominids, brainy and walking on two legs, began to alter natural objects to use as tools. Members of this species learnt to chip away at river pebbles and so create sharp-edged stones that they could use to butcher animals with. They would use bones as hammers and anvils to break apart other bones. This species was, in fact, the first to manufacture tools in a planned manner and became known scientifically as the genus Homo, meaning man. Sometime between 100,000 and 200,000 years ago, a new group within this genus appeared. It was different from any previous group of humans: less heavily built, more mobile with cognitive flexibility unknown before. This is the group of humans from which we are all descended. [ibid. p. 19.] "For tens of thousands of years, these anatomically modern humans - people who looked like us - stayed within the confines of the mother continent. Around 100,000 years ago one group of them made a foray into the Middle East, but was apparently unable to press onward. They needed an edge they did not have. Then, after 70,000 years ago, a small founder population broke out of Africa and began a more successful campaign into new lands." [Marean, C. "The most invasive Species of All" in Scientific American (August 2015) p. 35.] They are believed to have reached Europe between 44,000 and 41,000 years ago. [Wong, K. "Neandertal Minds" in Scientific American 312 (February 2015) p. 38.]   In the course of their expansion they encountered other closely related human species: the Neanderthals in western Europe (who had lived there since 350,000 years ago) and members of the recently discovered Denisovan lineage in Asia. "Like us, these people could envisage and desire new lands to explore and conquer. So they built ocean worthy vessels and set out across the sea, reaching Australian shore by at least 45,000 years ago … By about 40,000 years ago they … found and crossed a land bridge to Tasmania

... On the other side of the equator, a population of H. sapiens travelling northeast penetrated Siberia and radiated across the lands encircling the North Pole. Exactly when they finally crossed into the new world is a matter of fierce debate, but researchers agree that by around 14,000 years ago they broke these barriers. [Marean, C. "The most invasive Species" p. 33.] In short, these modern African humans populated the rest of the world. There has been a fierce debate going on as to whether these modern humans, our forefathers, exterminated every other human in their path or whether they actually interbred with them. For instance, did the modern African biped making his tools really kill off all Neanderthals in what is now central Europe, or did they interbreed, or did both these processes occur? Recent research seems to tend towards interbreeding, rather than exterminating. [Wong, K. Scientific American p. 43.]

147 Olson, S. Mapping Human History p. 14.
148 ibid.
149 Cronin, J. "Creole Cape Town" p. 50.
150 8 May 1996 in Cape Town.
151 Personal communication, Cornelia Limpricht.
152 Breckenridge, K. "The Book of Life" p. 228.
153 ibid. p. 227.
154 ibid. p. 230.
155 Verwoerd was the South African prime minister from 1961 to 1966 when he was assassinated. He is considered to be the master behind the engineering and implementing the apartheid laws of racial segregation in the country.
156 Being interested in the biological side of what made me what I am, I had myself tested. This is a very simple test for which you collect some saliva and send it off to a laboratory, which does this kind of analysis. My results showed that I belonged to Hapla Group B4.

www.ingramcontent.com/pod-product-compliance
Lightning Source LLC
Chambersburg PA
CBHW081740270326
41932CB00020B/3350

9 783905 758795